Knights of Madness

The Quest for Spiritual Truth

Adrian Holland

Published by AMAZOLA

The right of Adrian Holland to be identified as the Author of the work has been asserted by him in accordance with the Copyright, Design and Patents Act 1988.

Copyright © Adrian Holland 2012

ISBN 978-0-9559678-6-3

All rights reserved. No part of this publication may be reproduced, stored in a retrieval system, or transmitted in any form or by means, electronic, mechanical, photocopying, recording, or otherwise, without the prior permission of the publishers.

For further information please contact the official website at

www.amazolapublishing.com

A copy of this book is held at the British Library.

Cover design and illustrations by Adrian Holland

I was very close to both of my parents who were my best friends, and I have lost count of the number of happy times we shared, and all of the creativity and laughter. Like my beloved father Joe, my mother Margaret was so special, and my total inspiration. I would therefore like to dedicate this book to their memory.

Contents

Introduction 4

One 7

Two 11

Three 18

Four 25

Five 31

Six 46

Seven 54

Eight 59

Nine 65

Ten 74

Eleven 82

Twelve 85

Introduction

This book has been an amazing journey for me, and one which came out of an extraordinary set of circumstances. I had become involved in a healing centre and been offered training in Reiki - a system of natural healing which evolved in Japan. Over the previous two years or so, I had risen to the dizzy heights of *Reiki Master*, and volunteered my services along with other dedicated therapists to provide treatment to those on limited income. It felt good giving something freely, and all that was asked in return was for a small donation towards the centres costs, which was partially funded by various charities.

I must admit that becoming involved or even training in complementary medicine was the last thing that I ever envisaged for myself. It all started when I was diagnosed with M.E. (Myalgic Encephalomyelitis) following Glandular fever. I had also suffered an adverse reaction to antibiotics which in turn presented me with more than one near death experience. I had been in a bad way with sporadic paralysis, and had been really struggling for several years. Quite by chance Reiki found me, and offered me a way out of my illness. The circumstances around this and my life story up until now can be found in my book *A Way of Being – The Journey to Spiritual Enlightenment.*

There is little point in going over my story here, suffice to say that I was very grateful for the improvement in my health. There was however, one thing which despite my best efforts was still plaguing me. I had a fear of electric storms.

I had not long turned three, and it was in the early autumn of 1968. One of the local amateur football teams had managed to get into the FA Cup, and had drawn a lower league team. There had been a lot of excitement and my parents had taken me along to the game in my pushchair. We were at the front of the crowd, quite near the touchline, with a *birds eye* view.

Just after half time it started to rain and this quickly developed into a torrential thunderstorm. All of a sudden a thunder bolt shot out of the sky and struck a player right in front of me. He fell to the ground, and sadly the force was great enough to take his life. The match was abandoned, and I was taken home.

There is no way that a three year old can fully understand or indeed make any sense of such an incident, as thankfully witnessing someone being killed by a thunderbolt is quite unique. The only real understanding is the fact that whenever a rumble of thunder is heard, it triggers off the memory of what happened on that fateful day. Now being in my late thirties, I still carried those memories and just one distant rumble would instantly turn me into a nervous wreck. It was not only very embarrassing, but it meant that I was constantly living in fear. It was almost like suffering from shell shock, where any loud noise or flash of light would send my heart racing and my body wanting to dive for cover. It was now late spring, and after the first storm of the year I could stand it no longer. I needed help with my phobia!

Quite by chance a new therapist started working at the centre, and she was qualified in something called *hypnotherapy*.

I had never even heard of hypnotherapy, or understood much about it. My only thought was that it involved being hypnotised. My only experience of this was seeing an illusionist on television doing his stage act. He would get members of the audience to do embarrassing things in some sort of a trance, until he clicked his fingers returning them to normality. I was getting quite desperate now, so booked myself in with her in the hope that she would somehow be able to help me. I just hoped that she would be able to stop my fear, so that whenever I saw a flash of lightening or heard a rumble of thunder, I would be able to just ignore it and carry on with my life.

What actually happened was something so different to what I had expected that it did indeed change my life, but not in a way I could have ever imagined...

One

The afternoon of my appointment soon arose, and I found myself walking through the centre's doorway towards the reception desk. I was actually on time for once, and quite hopeful that in just under an hour's time, the new *me* would be walking out of the door phobia free!

After exchanging the usual pleasantries with the lady at reception, I was soon walking down the familiar carpet towards the door at the end of the corridor. It was ironic that in all of the time I had worked there, I had never used that particular room. Somehow, I had been kept away from it and now I was about to enter it for the very first time.

I knocked on the door and was met by an attractive lady with a shock of beautiful auburn hair. She had warm light blue eyes and a radiant smile. We shook hands and I was guided to a chair in the centre of the room.

There was more than a hint of embarrassment on my part as I explained all about my phobia, and the way it had been affecting my life. She tried to reassure me that I was not on my own as there are many people who also feel this way. There was even a Roman Emperor called *Caligula* who was ridiculed by Rome for hiding under the bed when there was a storm. However, being well over six feet tall and with a large build to go with it, my phobia did little for my self respect, as it was assumed that I would naturally be fearless. In many ways I was, but this was my proverbial *Achilles heel*.

She looked into my eyes and started asking me a series of questions, and naturally I started to tell her all about how my phobia started. Nothing seemed to be happening and I began to doubt whether I was being hypnotised at all. Maybe I was just going to have to live with it?

I felt a sense of disillusion filling my body, and so decided to get up.

However, when I tried to move, my body would not respond and instead of raising myself up off the chair, I suddenly found myself sitting in my pushchair as a three year old flanked by my beloved and soon to be late parents. We were in the crowd at the football match, right at the front, and I could hear the chanting and feel the excitement of the game. It seemed as though there were thousands of people there, all crammed into the tiny ground. It was quite loud as the players ran about chasing the football, as the referee blew his whistle for a foul, the noise of the crowd increased. I did not really understand what was going on, or why my parents had brought me here. My mind was full of questions as I felt a spot of rain on my face and looked up to see some dark clouds approaching, as my mother pulled the clear polythene rain cover over me.

A rumble of thunder echoed in the distance as I began to tense up, and I could clearly hear the voice of the hypnotherapist over the noise of the crowd. "And what happened next?"

I nearly jumped out of my skin, as a massive flash of lightening lit up the sky followed by a very loud crash of thunder. There seemed to be pandemonium and I could see a player rolling in agony on the ground as the referee and some of the players huddled around him. The rain was absolutely torrential now as the player suddenly stopped moving. Although I was only three, somehow I knew that he had died, which was soon confirmed by my parent's conversation.

I could feel my heart racing as I was consumed by fear, trapped half way between my distant memory and my current experience. It felt quite odd, to say the least, as my mouth worked on *auto pilot* with words flooding out, of which I seemed to have absolutely no control.

I could hear my voice talking about my grandmother. She was a lady of immense courage and wisdom. Lady was correct, as she walked away from the *Aristocracy* for love, and love in abundance is what she gave out, especially to me. Unfortunately she passed away just after my first birthday, and her principles, ethics and way of being have stayed with me ever since. Although so young, I just know that she had a profound affect on my life, and I carry her love and total admiration in my heart.

From somewhere deep in my subconscious mind I began to recall a conversation that I had with my mother. Apparently my grandmother also used to have a phobia of electric storms and in the days before we had a television, she used to put the radio outside in the rain in case it attracted lightening. My mother said that she used to shake and she was that bad that she made the dog shake too, and mother had both of them to deal with!

The hypnotherapist suggested that I meet my grandmother as she believed that in some way I had also picked up her fear and that if we discussed it then it would lift my phobia.

A sense of relief filled my body as I entered the *between state* again. A swirling white mist cleared and I could see her standing there on a river bank wearing a beautiful long dress, hat and gloves. It was before the *First World War* and she looked very elegant, being in her late teens. I felt a feeling of euphoric love emanating from her as she told me that there was nothing to fear, and that she loved me so very much.

I could feel a tear rolling down my cheek as the white mist reappeared which began to intensify as I entered a brilliant tube of light. It resembled a long triangular room shaped like a *toblerone*. My mother bought me one every Christmas and I relaxed sensing that I was completely safe in here. The room seemed to have doors on either side, and as I walked along I decided to open one of them. When I walked through, I found myself crouching in a beautiful garden. I was about six years of age and was fascinated by the plants. There was a very thin stemmed plant that reached up forming part of an arch with tiny delicate leaves. I gently put my fingers between the stem holding some of the leaves in my palm. I seemed to be captivated by it and hardly noticed a man approaching. When I looked up I could see that he was wearing a simple white robe, with the hood resting on his shoulders. He had a brown beard and long wavy brown hair, and as I looked into his eye I asked him why he was going to let them do to him what they were going to do. He just gave me the most enigmatic smile that again filled me with euphoric love.

I was now back in the *toblerone*, walking towards another door. This one revealed a scene of Ireland and somehow I had the date of 1919 in my mind. I was standing in a small cottage with a dirt floor, and as I looked out of the window I could see about half a dozen aircraft which looked like *Gypsy Moths*. The sight of them took me to a memory of flying over a battlefield with loud explosions and the horrors of trench warfare stretched out beneath me.

Everything suddenly changed as I hurried along a cobbled street wearing a *Royal Flying Core* uniform. I was only about nineteen and back in Ireland again and there was a lot of civil unrest. It was during the uprising, and as I turned the corner I could see some buildings which had already been destroyed. I was making my way towards a little café with yellow walls and little green windows. I had the feeling that I was in love with a lady who was inside, and that this would probably be the last time that I would ever see her.

The scene began to fade as I entered the *toblerone* again. It appeared that I was searching for something, as my subconscious mind wandered up and down. For some reason I stopped sensing that this particular doorway held whatever I had been searching for. Little did I realise who was waiting for me on the other side, or what an effect he would have on my life…

Two

The light glistened off the sword of his forefathers as Luke lashed out wildly with rage, born out of frustration rather than anger. Why was he always thrust into situations not of his own making, rather than being left in peace. Peace was all that he had ever wanted, and yet conflict followed him like an unwelcome companion. For longer than he could remember he had felt this way, and this morning's events were still welling up inside him. He let out a deafening roar just like a lion stalking his territory, although this particular lion had now been forced to leave his. He knew that his father was a good man at heart, and yet, being the second son, he always felt as though it should be his elder brother taking the lead. Looking back at the flames billowing out of the castle window perched high in the keep, he felt the pains of guilt rising into the air like the smoke rising in the distance. His father always described it as the rage of destiny, which burned in his soul and exploded when it was ignited. It had certainly been today, and those that knew him were keeping their distance until the waters of emotion finally quelled the raging fires within.

A rumble of thunder rang out across the prairie as even the gods shared in his frustration. More than anything he wanted to disappear into the mountain peaks with their swarthy layers of heather, but he knew that he would have to return to the castle, but not before he had come to terms with what had been said.

Luke held his sword up defiantly against the approaching storm, almost tempting the gods to strike him down with a thunderbolt, to finally put him out of his misery. He knew deep down that this was futile as they always protected him and he had a reputation of being invincible. This frustrated him even more, as he knew that death would bring him the peace that he desired.

Every battle that he had fought had been thrust upon him as justice reigned supreme in his soul. There was always someone in these unsettled times who crossed his path, seeking something they were not morally entitled to. Tyrants subjected the people to untold cruelties in the great lands of these islands, and it was as though they sought him out as some kind of a test, and he had lost count of the number he had dispatched. This had brought him rewards greater than most could imagine, and the more he tried to refuse them, or give them away, the more they had seemed to accumulate. Luke really hated power, and his father's kingdom had grown steadily, particularly over the past few years, due mainly to his conquests. He had never sought to conquer; it was just that the surrounding war lords had desired his father's kingdom and when defeated, their lands had fallen under his father's rule which now stretched from the mountains all the way to the great wall of the Romans.

Luke stopped resting for a moment as he tried to compose himself. Never before had he faced such a situation and, although he longed for sanctuary, he knew in his heart that it was his destiny to follow his father's orders. Looking up at the darkening sky he realised that, although in his heavy heart it was the last thing that he wanted to do, running away was not an option. He had never run away from anything, always meeting everything that had been forced upon him. If he did then, it was only a matter of time before events caught up with him. If he stayed on his father's land, he would be sought out and eventually brought back to his father; although he was a compassionate man for these times, he was the King and his word was law!

Reluctantly he turned around to head back towards the castle, and meet his fate, although there was one special place that he would be visiting before he embark on his journey.

Turning to face the impending storm he walked back towards the castle's white stone walls, which were silhouetted against the blackening skies. The first of the rain drops caught his face as the wind picked up, and the rain water was soon running down his body armour as he snorted through his helmet like a raging bull.

It was not long before he reached the river whose fast current cascaded down the valley, corralled by the lines of ancient trees and large rocky boulders that scoured their way into the prairie landscape. The river protected one side of the castle from invaders, who would be swept away if they were foolhardy enough to try and cross. Only the old Roman bridge offered safe passage, and that was heavily fortified, forming the castle's outer defences. There was, however, a secret entrance built by the same people who had originally constructed the fortress, which had become the castle when reoccupied years after it was abandoned. It was as a child that Luke had stumbled upon the trapdoor that concealed the lowest level of the vaults in the store house. Who would have thought that a simple childhood game would have opened up such possibilities as an adult?

Luke slipped along the narrow gap between the rock face and the river, between the boulders until he came to the one he knew so well. It had been a really good friend to him, hiding many of his secrets. Lying by the boulder was the trusted branch which he skilfully used to lever it to one side, revealing the fault in the rock face that was the entrance to the secret passageway. Although he had discovered it as a child, it had taken him many years to gain the strength to move the boulder, and it was only a few short years ago that he had managed to take advantage of his childhood discovery.

Luke knelt down, squeezing through the small opening until he was able to stand up on the other side. The light from outside was just enough for him to see the flint and torch that he had placed there to aid his accent into the very bowels of the castle. He skilfully struck the magical flints together until he produced the spark that lit his lantern. Now he could see the strong wooden ladder that he had constructed in secret, which led up to the trapdoor in the storehouse floor. He held one of only two keys, which again was another one of the castles secrets.

Holding the rungs with his strong left hand he began to climb, as the torch in his right hand illuminated his way. There were only about twenty rungs, but they were enough to bridge the void of the ancient chasm. He took the key from around his neck placing, it in the lock which grated as the lever slid to one side. Pushing against the large heavy wooden panel, it began to rise, just as he intended when he replaced the ancient timbers and rebuilt the platform in secret. It had not been easy, but being the king's second son, no one had dared question him. Respect was one of the few advantages of his position, and one of which he had never taken advantage of, well maybe just this once!

Luke pushed the trap door to one side before entering the storehouse. Inside were housed many of his personal things, including the chest that held his riches. Luke was, by anyone's standards, extremely wealthy, as the many conquests had brought him great rewards. However, unlike most people of this time, it all meant nothing to him. He had been so richly rewarded, and yet the rewards that he sought could not be purchased.

The torchlight fell over the other items securely stored away in this most secret of places. Together with the chest, wrapped in cloth were several books, which were his true treasure, along with various pieces of military equipment and a selection of jars containing the ingredients for the ancient medicines that would lead him to his destination.

Luke pulled on the little cord around his neck, which held another key to the door that would lead him to another secret passageway, the knowledge of which he shared with just one other person. The lock was quite stiff, although it did open with a little pressure, and then he was into the corridor whose steep steps led up to yet another door. This one was made of heavy oak and one of the keys to its lock was located behind a carved stone in the wall. It was so expertly done that it was almost impossible to detect, and with a little gentle persuasion he was able to remove it. The key was cold and slightly rusty, however he soon had it in the lock, and, again with a little effort, he was able to move the locking mechanism with a gentle *clunk*.

The door was quite heavy, but not to someone of his size and strength, and he soon pushed it to one side. Ahead of him the passageway stretched up steeply, carved out by an ancient stream, and expertly turned into a secret escape root by unknown craftsmen of the Roman occupation. Luke had to stoop as his considerable size almost filled the cramped space as he made his way towards yet another heavy oak door. This one just had the bolt on the inside, to aid an escape, preventing any pursuers from following.

Luke hauled the door open to reveal the back of a large tapestry which concealed the door from view, aiding the deception. He extinguished the torch, placing it in its iron holder bolted to the wall, before delicately pushing the tapestry to one side. He was now in an open stone room, and ahead of him lay a stone altar originally dedicated to a long forgotten Roman Goddess. The emerging sunlight which had broken through the black clouds of the now breaking storm cast three distinct shadows from the large arched windows, as a distant rumble of thunder echoed down the valley. The only other sound was that of the cascading water which rushed passed on the other side, heading towards the Roman bridge.

The room was now dedicated to a new set of Gods and Goddesses of the pagan tradition, which in turn were close to being replaced by the God of the new religion which had now taken hold. Before too long they would also be consigned to history, and in time be forgotten along with their predecessors. Simply laid out with candles and flowers placed on an ornately woven cloth, the altar was the only thing inside apart from a simple rug and kneeling stool. Moving silently towards the door on the far side, past the main door which led to the castle, he noticed that it was firmly bolted indicating that the sole occupant was in residence.

The far door was unlocked and Luke was able to open it with ease, and a blast of warm air greeted him which contrasted to the chill of the main room. A simple fire illuminated the inside, casting shadows over the table which held a collection of jars, a pestle and mortar and several books. There was a clink as his sword caught the stone floor when he removed it from his left shoulder, placing it by the bed. Someone stirred beneath the blankets which draped over the bed as a soft voice exclaimed "Is that you Luke?"

This was the first hint of affection directed at him for what seemed like days, and the voice echoed the fire whose warmth gladdened his aching heart.

"Yes!" Luke whispered as he removed his wet body armour, revealing his muscular torso, silhouetted against the far wall. Luke was an enormous man, standing well over six feet tall, with thick long black wavy hair that cascaded down to his shoulders and a thick beard indicating the best part of a week's growth. He bent down to unclasp his boots before removing his trousers and slipping beneath the warm blankets.

"You're cold!" The gentle voice exclaimed as a set of arms wrapped themselves around his broad shoulders. "I've missed you and I don't want you to go!"

Luke frowned with frustration. This was an impossible situation, and it was this frustration that had boiled over earlier causing his rage. He felt incensed and his mind drifted back to when he had stormed out of the castle. He had never been so angry in his whole life and his muscles tensed as he relived it all over again. It had been quite hard to breathe in his helmet and his body armour felt heavy as he stormed up towards the distant mountains. The great sword of his grandfather made his left shoulder ache and he was struggling to get his breath. It suddenly felt very hot and stuffy inside his armour, and when he heard the rumble of thunder, he held the great sword up and bellowed out at the top of his voice.

Three, two, one…

I opened my eyes to see the hypnotherapist standing over me looking very concerned. I was gasping for breath and sweating profusely.

"Are you OK?"

For a few moments I did not know where I was, or for that matter who I was!

I was in a daze and nearly fell over when I tried to get to my feet. My legs seemed to have a mind of their own, and as for my mind, it seemed to have been taken over by a very angry black night!

It took her several minutes to settle me down, and I do not remember any of our conversation. It was only on my walk home that I began to calm down, and when I finally reached the front door my only thought was of my bed. I do remember laying there wondering just what had just happened to me, and fortunately sleep beckoned which came as a great relief!

Three

That evening and much of the following day were spent talking to my wonderful mother. She always gave me good council and suggested that it was about time that I distanced myself from the centre. She told me that I had never been the same since I had become involved with it, and that all of this was not doing me any good. She certainly had a point, as it had changed me - I was now experiencing the life of someone else, and not the most contented one at that!

I did go to see the hypnotherapist the following week, and had several other visits over the next month. We did a lot of talking and her advice was that I was unique (as are we all) and not to change. However, she also advised me that it would take a very understanding person to share my life, and particularly my recent experiences!

Never was a truer word spoken, as I felt as if I was out of step with myself. If I did share my recent experiences with someone, then they would probably think that I was delusional. I longed for normality, and to be able to fit in with *normal* people. The whole business had shaken me to the very core, however there was an even greater shock awaiting me...

A few weeks later my life suddenly changed dramatically with the loss of my beloved father. He really was an extraordinary man, and someone I always looked up to with deep respect and admiration. Words can not convey his outstanding qualities and the effect he had on my life and those that he touched with his compassion, wisdom, and a presence that made everyone feel at ease. Being twice the size and four times the strength of the average man, his gentle ways and the love that he gave I will cherish for the rest of my life. (This part of my life is also documented in my book *A Way of Being - The Journey to Spiritual Enlightenment*).

I had no further encounters with Luke over the next twelve months as my wonderful mother and myself struggled to come to terms with life without the great man by our side.

I did continue to undertake a little work at the centre, and also attended a few courses which gave me a welcome distraction. Following one of them I was invited out to the cinema by some people I had became friendly with. They were excited about a new film, and so I accepted their invitation and they very kindly picked me up in their car. What was planned as a relaxing evening out provided me with a lot more than I bargained for...

The film was the last in the *Lord of the Rings* trilogy. I must have been the only person in the whole country who had not heard of the books or films. My new friends could not believe it, and told me that I was in for quite an experience - I certainly was, as they were about to find out!

The film started and I began to feel very uncomfortable, I was very edgy and felt similar to when there was a thunder storm forecast. The film appeared to be very good, but I just wanted to leave as this strange feeling began to spread through my body. It was almost like static building up inside me, and as soon as the character of the King appeared on screen with his long black wavy hair and beard I felt myself slipping into a swirly white mist which soon developed into the familiar looking brilliant white *toblerone*.

Luke lay wrapped around his lover, although she was far more than just a conquest. They had always been close even as children and their love had been forbidden as she was little more than an outcast in this new society. For many years a *medicine woman* had commanded great respect, and in real terms had been regarded as second only to the king, but now in these changing times such a person was regarded with fear and in some ways as little more than the *devil incarnate*.

People used to live at one with nature and the four elements believing that everything had its own spirit. They had a desire to connect with these *spirits,* and at the head of all of these spirits sat *Mother Nature,* the *Mother Goddess.* A medicine woman was the connection to these spirits and it was to her that people turned for healing and guidance. They also used to refer to her as the carrier of the *Divine Feminine,* and that role had now been taken over by *Mary Magdalene.* Crusaders were everywhere pledging their allegiance to her and had taken up the cross, going off to the *Holy Land* on *pilgrimages.* All of their property was placed under the protection of the new Church of Rome, which was rapidly becoming the main power of the land.

The embrace progressed into passionate love making as they united as one, as they had done many times over the past few years. Their pledges to one another had been performed in secret under the old ways. This union would not have been sanctified by the Church, and particularly not by the King, who was in a difficult position as the sheer power wielded by Rome was far greater than any king could muster. He had decreed that his second son seek knowledge of these new ways in an attempt to protect his kingdom. There was no way that Luke would take up the cross, despite going against the will of the King, who would not sanction his elder son as he feared his lands would be taken over by the church, and so Luke had been chosen. There had been a mighty disagreement with Luke kicking over a brazier, setting fire to the castle, as his ranging temper was vented like the inferno that he had created. Fortunately there had only been superficial damage, but it had rocked the castle and every one of its occupants. Being a mighty warrior had in some way protected Luke as there were few brave enough to stand in his way, particularly when he had such rage inside. Now however, his fires had turned to burning desire, which raged on until they were finally extinguished.

Luke rolled onto his back as he thought of all that had happened, and wished that he and his beloved could just disappear into the night. His father's realm stretched all the way to the sea, and on either side lay hostile kingdoms, whose rulers he had already done battle with. There would certainly be no welcome for him there, and for the first time in his life he felt trapped. Being the King's son he had enjoyed a lot of freedom, but sadly those days were now over. The King had already made arrangements for his safe passage to the Holy Land, and a sizeable fee had been paid. Even if he were to attempt to slip away, the King had many allies and word would soon reach him. He looked across to the delicate bundle huddled under the blankets fearing what would happen to her if the King's wrath was vented. They were both lucky that his patronage had extended this far, which was more than most medicine women had received. They had been persecuted, or even worse, executed for their ancient wisdom. Times were changing and Luke sighed, realising that it was a *fête accompli*.

There was a stirring beneath the blankets and he felt a delicate hand caress his broad chest. Why did he have to go off to the Holy Land to seek *Divine Unity*, when he had already found it?

In his mind Luke was already beginning to prepare himself to leave. At least he had not taken any vows, otherwise he may not have had the opportunity to return until he fulfilled all that the church would have decreed. He had already seen many leave and not return, and he was determined not to be one of them. It was different for him as he did not believe in the same way as the others, who would willingly sacrifice their lives for the *new ways*. He was a man of the *old ways*, and to him it made no real difference who controlled Jerusalem. His God existed everywhere, in everything which was holy. Luke was a man of peace, although war seemed to follow him wherever he went. His crusade was one of freedom and he had grown tired of conflict despite having dispatched many adversaries in his life. When he thought back, he could not remember a single occasion where he had sought conflict. There was only one person who knew his real nature and had felt his gentleness, and she was lying beside him.

The fires were beginning to die down, not just in him, but also in the stone fireplace which was providing them with warmth. He gently slipped the delicate hand to one side before carefully emerging from the thick blankets, moving across the room and sending a shadow out across the solid wooden door. His skin gratefully received the heat from the flames as his naked flesh rippled with muscle. Fortunately there were many logs stacked to one side of the fireplace, and he began to stack the fire, which would keep burning until morning. He would think of this fire many times on his long journey and its warmth along with the warmth, in his heart for the one who held his soul he knew would sustain him. The logs began to crackle as the flames burnt off the moisture of the bark, and a spark fell into the grating. He took this as a sign that he would return, and he knew that as long as the fire burnt inside him that he would have the resolve to overcome whatever he encountered.

Luke relaxed as dusk fell over the castle, and his mind wandered back towards a poignant childhood memory. He would only have been about six years of age when the old medicine woman returned from one of the surrounding villages. She had a young girl of similar age with her, and there were looks of disdain in the child's eyes. It was customary for all medicine women, when they reached a certain age, to go forth and seek a girl child to train in the ancient ways that had served the people so well for longer than anyone could remember. Her power, however, was waning, as were the powers of all of the other medicine women who still practised. It was a dying art, as the new religion had already replaced most of them. She might even have been cast out herself, if it had not been for her healing powers, which had saved the King's life.

The King had fallen ill and developed a fever which had threatened to take his life. The medicine woman had stayed by his side for three days and three nights until the fever had broken, and in return he had given her his patronage, and decreed that by his command she would be allowed sanctuary. This had also been extended to her young apprentice who stood there frightened and alone. She had been taken from her family as she had demonstrated a natural ability in the ways of the ancient ones. Luke remembered smiling at her, as there was just something different about her. This had developed into a strong friendship which had blossomed over the years. They had been virtually inseparable as children, and he had also learnt many of the *old ways* too, becoming skilled in the ancient arts. It had given him that vital edge in battle, although a life of battle was something that he longed to change. Change was rapidly approaching, however, and not of the kind he sought.

Placing another log on the fire, he turned to look at the bed feeling, the warmth on his back as he looked longingly at the small bulge in the blankets. This was something else that he would take with him, and whenever he saw a fire, or wrapped himself in a blanket he would think of this moment. He crept silently across the stone floor, slipping back under the blankets without a sound. For a very big man he was incredibly light on his feet and this combined with his strength and agility, made him a worthy opponent for any possible adversary. Conflict was however for tomorrow, for the rest of the day had been set aside for *Divine Unity*.

There was a brief movement as arms wrapped themselves around him, holding him tight as if they were never going to let him go. She too would think of this moment and whenever she slept, she would imagine that she was nestled under his strong powerful arm cradling his large muscular torso.

The sun had finally set and with it his old life, dawn would bring the start of a new one, but for now the sands of time were on their side.

"Adrian!"

I sat there in a daze half sensing that there were people standing over me.

"It's time to go."

I stared up through unseeing eyes, as I felt a hand on my arm. It was no use as I was still in that place between *here* and *there*.

"What's wrong with him?"

There was a conversation about me going on, and I felt several other pairs of hands trying to haul me out of my seat. My legs had turned to jelly, and I tottered precariously along the isle and out into the foyer. They sat me down on a seat and it took them half an hour to get me to the car. There was a mixture of concern and amusement as I stared blankly out of the window.

Before long we arrived at the house of two of my new friends, and still a little dazed, I staggered up the driveway and into the lounge. They belonged to a *medieval re-enactment society*, and the first thing that I saw were two replica swords. I instantly picked them up and started displaying my swordsmanship.

"These are a lot lighter than my swords." I exclaimed nearly taking the light fitting off the ceiling. Fortunately I was persuaded to hand them over, and still feeling a bit faint I decided to head towards the bathroom, much to the relief of everyone. Once inside I filled the wash basin with cold water and stuck my head in it. It was so refreshing and I felt myself returning to *normal*. I lifted my head, looked into the mirror and screamed, for there staring back at me was the reflection of a man with dark black wavy hair and black beard, wearing boiled black leather armour.

Suffice to say that after being given a cold drink I was promptly dropped off at my home. The strange thing was that I was not invited out by them again!

Four

I decided to keep my new experience to myself, feeling that instead of regression therapy, what I really needed was psychotherapy!

Several months passed as I kept a low profile, supporting my wonderful mother and concentrating on my artwork. I was very thankful for the normal everyday things such as the big weekly shop, and this particular week appeared to be the same as usual, and so off to the supermarket we went. During our visit I happened to wander into the DVD section, and there in the new releases I spotted the film I had been taken to see. I frowned as I picked up the empty case, remembering what an exhibition I had made of myself. Studying the picture on the front of the man in armour with the black wavy hair and beard I decided that it was probably better to put it back and walk away from the whole experience. I was just about to move when a small boy of about eight years of age nudged me on the leg pointing to the sword on the cover.

"It looks as though you are going to take someone's head off with that!"

I went pale!

If I had not have known any better, I would have sworn that he could see me standing there as Luke, the angry black night!

It must have been several months after that I received a telephone call from one of my old friends. She worked for a travel company based near Manchester airport, and was just wondering how I was getting along. I must admit to briefly talking about my *experience* with her, which was probably why she had not been in touch for a while!

She had some free tickets to a theme park, which had come courtesy of her employers, which involved an overnight stay. I was informed that it would be separate beds and *no funny business*. Little did she realise how those words were going to come back to haunt her!

I drove to her house in Manchester and we set off in her car. The conversation was quite normal until we approached the theme park. There was a big sign directing us to the next exit, and as we looked at it she suddenly realised where we were heading; *Camelot!*

For some reason she had not made any connection, and now I received a rather strange look. Neither of us commented, although I could sense her trepidation. We soon found the car park and I grabbed the luggage as we headed off towards the hotel. The first thing that I noticed was Pemberton Street - *Pemberton* was the maiden name of my grandmother on my father's side. Then there was a sign for *Holland's pies* which made me feel at home as there is apparently a distant family connection. My friend also knew this and gave me one of those looks, without saying a word. Then as we approached the area where they do the *medieval re-enactments*, the men who were dressed in armour lined up, placing their hands on the hilts of their swords and bowing as I walked past!

My friend nearly dropped her bag, shaking her head in disbelief.

The day was very pleasant, with a lovely evening meal and a few drinks - purely for medicinal purposes on my friend's part! It did seem to settle her down and it was not long before we decided to retire for the evening.

My bed was quite comfortable, and it was not long before I drifted off to sleep…

———

The sound of footsteps echoed across the great hall as the King marched in from his chambers. It was going to be a mixed blessing sending his second son off on a journey of discovery to the *Holy Land*. He knew that he had little choice, as he needed greater knowledge of what lay behind this new religion as he struggled with the transition from the *old ways* to the *new*. There was such great pressure in these times, and although he was indeed a very powerful man, he knew that there were even greater forces out there as the whole of ancient Briton struggled to form its own identity after the fall of the Roman Empire. It was rumoured that there was a powerful king, whose lands lay far to the south, who sought to unify the whole land, and the King was concerned about the future. He felt that at his age he lacked the drive and energy to face such a challenge, which would lie in the hands of his sons. He could not spare his eldest, so the only one who could provide him with a first hand account was Luke. There was no one else he really trusted to fulfil this mission, and he realised that Luke's lack of enthusiasm would mean that he was not going to get caught up in the euphoria that had engulfed many a pilgrim, and knight alike.

There was a degree of sadness in his heart, as it was always difficult for a father to say farewell to his son, particularly one who had served him so well. He could credit him for strengthening his kingdom and subduing his enemies. Land and wealth had also been accumulated and he was now regarded as one of the most powerful men in these lands. Sending his son would also strengthen his position as there had been talk, mostly spread by the new church, that by not sending his knights on a crusade he was betraying God.

The king was a wise man and understood what really lay at the heart of this new church. It was all about power and money, and establishing trade routes, as well as getting rid of anyone who did not follow this new faith.

He paced up and down anxiously waiting for Luke to emerge, hoping that today's encounter would not be as hostile as the one they had the day before. The castle still had blackened walls and although he was the King, like everyone else, he feared his second son's power and skill as a warrior. He knew that his son would not harm him, but to see him in such a temper was enough to shake him as well as the castle to the very foundations.

The King felt a presence in the room and turned to see Luke standing there. He was startled as he did not hear him enter. This was typical of Luke as he was like a ghost when he moved. In all his years he had never known anyone with the ability to move so silently. He was proud of his son, and the fact that he had trained Luke in the same way his own father had trained him many years ago. Luke, however, was not the most willing of students and it had taken him many years to change the gentlest of children into a battle ready warrior. He had always been so comfortable living in his brother's shadow, and the two boys were completely different. His eldest was born to be King, and had a commanding presence about him. He was just as fair as Luke was dark, and there was little resemblance between them. He knew that they were both his sons, although they acted so differently.

There was an uneasy silence until the king spoke.

"Luke!"

"Sire!" Luke replied, awaiting his orders, which he knew would be coming.

"I have arranged passage on a ship destined for the *Holy Land*, and I have also arranged an escort to get you safely to the coast, which is only a day's ride from here."

Luke nodded, bowing to the inevitable.

"I know that you are unhappy with my orders, but as King and your father, you will obey my will!" This sounded harsh, but the more gentle approach of yesterday had resulted in the only real disagreement that the two men had ever had. This had really hurt both of them and there had been more than a little testosterone flowing through their veins.

"Adrian!"

The white mists returned interrupting Luke and his father.

"You're talking in your sleep!"

The white mists continued to swirl for a few moments before clearing again...

———

From the brow of the hill the countryside stretched out in the distance, rolling gently down towards the sea. The muddy path undulated as it twisted and turned towards the little fishing village which sat huddled against the coast line, with its assortment of stone and wooden buildings surrounding the small stone jetty. The safety of the castle walls lay several miles behind, as the unknown world stretched out like the ultimate *leap of faith*. It must have been the same for all who had trodden this path, and there were other pilgrims who were also about to make the journey to the *Promised Land*. He could see them sporadically dotted along the path heading in the same direction. Luke had visited this village several times in the past, although the purpose of his last visit was a far cry than the one he was making today. It would be nightfall in only a few hours, and they needed to get to the settlement before the sun set over the distant horizon.

These were still troubled times, and even though this was his father's kingdom it was not wise to camp out at night without a significantly larger escort. Luke feared no one, although he realised that the horses had become tired and they needed resting.

———

"Adrian!!!"

This time the mists cleared quickly to reveal my exasperated friend standing over me.

"You're keeping me awake!"

Apparently I had been deep in conversation with myself, much to her annoyance, and I got the feeling that I had stretched our friendship a little too far. Having a dream is one thing, but when you are having visions and giving a running commentary, on top of acting more than a little oddly for some time...

I lay awake for a while thinking about Luke. It really was strange how, every now and then, something would trigger a little bit more of his story. It was fascinating looking at the world through someone else's eyes, particularly as it all felt so real. I appeared to have all of his senses and could actually feel the wind on my face and smell the sweat of the horses. It really was as though I was there, experiencing everything for myself, and what had started out as an attempt to rid myself of my phobia had turned into a virtual reality experience.

I did not seem to have any control over the visions, and somehow they were connected with the people who crossed my path. I would never have come to this theme park if I had not been invited, or gone to see that film either. There seemed to be strange forces at work, although my behaviour was not *normal* in the eyes of my friends, who, for some reason, had begun to distance themselves from me!

This happened to be the last time that I saw this particular friend, but it was not the last time that I encountered Luke...

Five

Several months later I was feeling generally run down. There was nothing in particular, just an accumulation of things. I had been working hard on my artwork, getting my first deck of angel cards together. There were seventy eight in all, and it had proved to be a mammoth task. My wonderful mother's health had started to deteriorate and we both missed my beloved father so very much. I had just returned from a *Mind, Body and Spirit* show where I had been exhibiting and selling my artwork. To my surprise I had encountered my original Reiki Master, who I had not seen him for six months. He was full of news about the centre and asked me if I would like go back. I must admit to feeling a little guilty as I should really have continued volunteering. I had just needed a break, and maybe it was time that I went back. He also suggested that I went for a treatment, and so I had booked myself in for the following day.

Everything had changed since my last visit, and the centre had undertaken a bit of a face lift. There were many new volunteers, and one of them was to be my therapist for the next hour. I followed her down the familiar corridor and before long I was lying on the couch as the relaxing music started to fill the room...

The clouds parted and the sun blazed its fiery red glow over the sea, as if God himself was showing his displeasure at the prospect of being disturbed by the ship that was now sailing towards the land which lay far beyond the horizon.

Luke followed the old ways and to him *God* was the *Green Man,* a consort of the *Mother Goddess* and the symbol of male energy. He represented the union of the *Divine* and the animal, and was depicted as having horns. The Horned God was the Lord of life, death and the underworld, and was the *Sun* to the

Goddess' *Moon*. He alternated with the Goddess in ruling over the fertility cycle of birth, death and rebirth, and was born at the winter solstice. He was united with the Goddess in marriage at *Bealtaine* (the midpoint in the sun's progress between the spring equinox and the summer solstice) and died at the summer solstice to bring fertility to the land as the *Sacred King*. To the others journeying with him, the *Green Man* represented the *Devil*, which was no coincidence as the new religion had been striving to replace the old ways, and in this way it could turn the people away from them. To Luke the male energy itself was the *Sun* or *Sacred King* and *Lord of Life*, and not some mythical man who bore a striking resemblance to the Roman king of the Gods *Jupiter*, or his Greek counterpart *Zeus*, whom he had read about as a child. The King had insisted that his sons were educated and had assigned scribes to teach them, even providing a small library of books which set him apart from many of his adversaries who could neither read or write.

Luke had also spent time with the medicine woman, and had learnt about the ancient ways of his people, which had been recorded in countless stories passed down from a long lost age. He had many questions in his mind, as the *Mother Goddess* seemed a much more natural source of eternal power than its new male counterpart. In his understanding, it all began when some men desired power and began to create a myth, which was the concept of the *rotten apple*. They knew that some children just turn out *bad*, despite everyone's best efforts, and so a myth about a *rotten child* began to take shape. It was described in an ancient scroll, which the medicine woman had shown him many years ago.

One day the Mother Goddess brought forth a boy child who turned out to be no good, despite all the mother's best efforts. He desired her throne and tried to overthrow her. It was too much for the loving, forgiving mother and the boy was banished forever, but continued to show up in disguise, sometimes posing as the mother herself.

The myth caused concern amongst the men, who now became uncertain as to whether the Goddess they were worshipping was in fact the *bad child* in disguise. Some of these men then became angry that the women did not take their fears seriously, and eventually, over time some of these men rebelled.

It was not difficult to create this myth, or to convince women of its possibility. It was easy to accept that if there were to be a *bad child*, then it would probably be a *boy,* as men had been considered inferior, and this child was referred to as *Satan* or the *Devil.*

Women were still deemed superior for their wisdom, insight, compassion and thinking, where as brute strength was a masculine trait. Luke had plenty of that, and could see the logic that the only one to have the physical strength to protect the *Goddess* and overpower this *evil one* would be another male.

A male *God* was now created whom he had read about in the book of mythical tales his father had acquired. This book had stories of *Gods* who were given greater roles, and the need for strength and protection began to replace the need for wisdom and love. Some of these Gods had enormous powers and quarrelling and fought for *Goddesses of Unspeakable Beauty,* creating the concept of *jealousy*. It was not long before this *jealousy* began to spread, and people began to believe that they must love the most powerful of these jealous Gods, or face his wrath.

There were other stories of those who resisted this *God of Wrath,* as the feminine Goddess's tolerant love of a mother for a child was now replaced by jealousy, wrath, intolerance and the demanding love of the new masculine God. On the altar of his secret love sat a small statue of the smiling Goddess experiencing limitless love, gently submitting to the laws of nature. This was in complete contrast to the stern looking God depicted by the monks in their texts, which he had also read, proclaiming power over the laws of nature, limiting love.

Luke, like the majority of the people in the northern half of theses lands, could trace his origins back to the *Norse* people who had settled all over Northern Europe. His own family came from the *Germanic* tribes, and even those who had recently conquered the south of these lands were *Norse* in origin. They were of the new religion, similar in that respect to the king who they had replaced, as it gained a *foot hold*. Trade and settlement was the main reason for conversion, and now he found himself isolated and under pressure to change. Looking around, he realised that he would probably be one of the only ones not to follow this new religion and be part of this crusade, and this would undoubtedly lead to confrontation. He was the only man of arms not to wear the white tunic with the red cross emblazoned on it. Some people had already looked at him with suspicion, and he longed to be back home with his secret love.

The air was fresh and ruffled his beard as the sails billowed above his head, carrying shouts from the crew as they tacked into the wind. The deck was a little cramped, and even more so below, so he moved up to the platform used by the archers in sea battles. He remembered tales of the long ships used by his forefathers which had sailed as far as *North America,* told in the sagas of the great halls. They would have been asking *Ran* the goddess of the sea to spare them, along with the god *Aegar*. She could lure unsuspecting ships to the rocks, where he could send high waves to capsize them. It would have been from the mighty *Odin* King of the Gods that they would have sought a blessing, although there was another blessing being sought. Beside him knelt a holy man praying to the God of the new religion.

The man suddenly raised his head, and looking straight into Luke's eyes he spoke.

"Have you come to pray, my son?"

This was the farthest thing from Luke's mind, and he was just about to dismiss this request when he felt himself kneeling besides the holy man. He just felt compelled as there was something different about this man. He gave off a wonderfully relaxed energy that was in complete contrast to that of all of the other so called *holy men* he had met before. They were all touched with arrogance, and were convinced that they were speaking on behalf of the new god, despite doing things that seemed at odds with the teachings of their prophet *Jesus*. Luke although far from being one of those from new religion, had nothing but respect for this man, and his teachings. In some way it felt as though they were not a million miles away from his own.

Luke's mind was already drifting as he thought about all the things that he had read from the book of the new religion. His father has insisted that he took it along with him, although he had many reservations. It was a small leather bound hand scribed version, created by a nameless monk in a long forgotten monastery. He had obviously dedicated his life to this new religion, as had the holy man kneeling next to him.

Luke was very sensitive to *energies*, as in his beliefs everything carried its own *energy* and was alive in its own way. He sought a oneness with everything, and, for the first time on his journey he began to feel at peace. There was something completely different about this holy man who appeared to be pure of spirit, and as he knelt there, Luke could feel many thoughts filling his mind. It was as though he was having a vision, which was something that he had only really experienced with the medicine woman and his secret love.

Through his closed eyes, Luke could see a massive golden dome perched high upon a hill in some far off land. He could see himself kneeling under its roof at an altar. It seemed to be a place of sanctuary, a place far away from space and time, where a man could be alone with his thoughts and connect to the great spirit which ruled over the cosmos. He felt drawn deeper and deeper into his vision as other thoughts entered his mind, and as he journeyed, he became completely unaware of the ship he was sailing on, or the holy man who knelt at his side.

Luke sought peace, and in this moment he touched a kind of peace that he hardly knew existed. It was as though he was being guided, and whoever the holy man was, he was incredibly powerful. Luke must have remained there for quite some time, for when he eventually opened his eyes the holy man had gone.

Luke got to his feet, eager to speak with this man as he had many questions, but he was nowhere to be seen. There were only two other passengers on the deck besides the members of the crew who were going about their business. Luke approached the passengers who had been standing at the foot of the steps and when he asked them about the holy man, they told him that they had been standing there for some time and that he had been the only one there. Luke found this hard to believe, but they insisted that they had watched him walk past them, kneel down and pray alone.

Luke was dumbfounded and did not believe them, for his experience was very real, and he just assumed that they were not telling him the truth, so he began to question the crew, who gave him a similar response. Luke did not believe them either and began a systematic search of the ship, but wherever he looked and whoever he asked, it appeared that there was no such holy man on board. This was quite a mystery!

I briefly reappeared in the therapy room as the soft music played in the background. The smell of incense began to fill my nostrils as I carefully opened an eye. There, working at my feet, was the therapist, busily concentrating on what she was doing. I felt as puzzled as Luke, wondering just who and what the holy man was.

I was now drifting somewhere between *here* and *there*, briefly reappearing into Luke's world for a moment and then back into my own. I could see him from a distance as I hovered like an eagle above him, and then above myself. I had never done this before, and somehow felt separated from each of us. I could see him busily searching for the holy man, as the voyage seemed endless, and then see myself becoming restless. I was mumbling something as the therapist looked up from her position at my feet. This seemed to unsettle her too, and she quickly finished off what she was doing. She was now standing by my side with a mixture of concern and amusement on her face. I already had a reputation for acting a little *oddly,* to say the least and my reputation quickly grew as I sat bolt upright, pointed to the wall and said "Holy Man".

A look of shock now filled her face, as I lay back down on the couch and started snoring. I could actually hear myself grunting away, and this was the first time that I realised that I did in fact snore!

This was quite embarrassing as I could not move a muscle, and made even more bizarre as I was standing next to the therapist, looking at myself cringing as she began to smile. Fortunately she found it quite amusing, and after seeing that I was comfortable, much to my relief left the room.

I am sure that many people have *out of body* experiences and I am no stranger to them, although they have mostly been concerned with my former illness, when I was seriously ill. I remained at my bedside looking at myself soundly asleep on the therapy couch, wondering if this was the pivotal moment when I crossed the line of *mental illness*. If this was the case, then how could I go to see my already exasperated doctor and explain. He was extremely sceptical of *complementary* medicine, preferring his list of prescription drugs. He had already prescribed anti-depressants, as my illness had been diagnosed as a mental and not physical one. Fortunately today, M.E. is recognised as a physical illness usually brought about by a serious viral infection - *Post Viral*

Fatigue Syndrome. Ironically it was prescription drugs, and my reaction to them that had caused my illness in the first place. I began to think that if I did explain all about Luke, then he would probably prescribe himself the antidepressant!

I only ever took one, which made me feel a whole lot worse. It increased my feeling of fatigue and left me feeling depressed!

I took them back to the doctors, to be met by a look of dismay as he put them in a drawer of his desk. I often wondered whether he would open it again after my appointments. It really was an uneasy relationship as my burgeoning file of failures grew on each visit. He had tried and failed to get me better, and so after about a dozen visits, had more or less given up on me. This is when the complementary, or in my case *alternative* therapy had taken over. It had made a real difference to my physical condition, and my mental - well apart from the visions and strange behaviour!

The port of Lisbon beckoned, giving Luke a temporary relief from the endless waves and the cramped conditions on-board ship. After a brief respite, he would be off to Marseilles, Sardinia, Sicily, Crete, Cyprus, and then finally Jerusalem. It was going to take him four months to finally reach his destination, and he felt like setting fire to the ship as he had done the castle!

Lisbon had not long been taken from the *Moors*, and their Arabic influence was everywhere. However, it was Luke's own influence onboard ship that had been causing problems. There was a tension in the air, as his attitude and behavior had caused a lot of resentment with both the passengers and crew. Being a knight of noble blood, his refusal to wear the cross whilst journeying to the Holy Land was seen as *blasphemy*. His bad temper had not helped the situation either, and it had taken the Captain's intervention to stop everything from boiling over. Fortunately the King's influence and money had been enough, although this had been stretched to the limit. The approaching port was the answer to everyone's prayers, and it would be with a huge sigh of relief on everyone's part when he finally disembarked.

The harbor stretched out before them as the ship approached the stone quay which reached out to greet them. It was not long before the ship was safely tethered up and the gangplank lowered, connecting them to land for the first time in weeks.

Luke gathered up his things and was one of the first to disembark. It felt good standing on firm stone instead of the constant rocking of the ship. He swayed a little as his legs got used to not having to cope with the motion of the ship. He looked round at the hustle and bustle of the busy port, his eyes scanning the people scurrying about as they went about their daily business. There were many traders moored up alongside several crusader ships, which were readying themselves for the journey to the *Holy Land*. This journey was the last thing that Luke had in mind, as he felt the pangs of hunger rippling around his stomach. The meager rations onboard ship were in no way sufficient to fill a man of his size, and he yearned for a hearty meal.

Luke pushed his way through the crowd, his eyes searching for any sort of a tavern. There was a street which lay directly in front of him and he instinctively headed towards it, hoping to find somewhere to eat. It was not long before he found a suitable establishment, with its little sign swinging gently in the breeze. It was with a sense of great relief as he bent forward, ducking under the low doorway, poking his head inside.

The sight that greeted him was a collection of tables and chairs which were for the most part full of an assortment of people. Some just drinking, whilst others were eating a variety of foods. It looked quite different from the taverns back home, although as long as they served food that was of little interest to him.

Luke made his way to the bar, and stuck a coin down on the wooden surface. This gained the attention of the man on the other side, who quickly produced a tankard, filling it with wine.

"Food!" Luke spoke for the first time and, looking at him, the man beckoned over a serving wench who showed him to a table.

Luke looked fearsome as hunger raged in his stomach, with his black boiled leather armor hugging his large muscular body. He was considerably bigger than anyone else the tavern keeper had seen, and with the giant sword of his grandfather slung over his left shoulder, this was one customer he was not going to offend!

"Food!" Luke pulled out his grandfather's sword forcing it down into the timbers of the floor, before placing his black helmet on the hilt. He had his black metal armor slung over his right shoulder along with the black leather bag which contained his belongings, and he placed them down on the floor next to the sword. Other customers looked round at him; their eyes popping as he lowered himself down onto the chair.

The atmosphere became tense as he took off his large black leather gauntlets placing them down on the table with a thud. Luke was hungry and very frustrated, and could barely contain the seething rage he felt inside. He had been angered by the others onboard ship, and vowed there and then not to set foot on it ever again under any circumstances. If he was going to journey to the *Holy Land,* then he would be doing it under a different mode of transport.

Luke was not a natural sailor, although it was better sailing than spending an extra few weeks travelling by horseback. He may have felt differently if he had not received constant pressure from the others, some of whom questioned why he did not wear the cross of the crusaders. They knew as well as he that, if he chose to, he could have quite easily dispatched them all, but the last thing that he wanted was to become a fugitive charged with a massacre. The church was powerful enough, and he realised that although he was a mighty warrior, even he was not mighty enough to defeat an entire army.

Food arrived quickly in the form of a large slab of bread and a plate of meat. Luke grabbed a leg of what he thought was mutton, although that did not seem to matter as he was so hungry that he could have easily eaten the leg of the table. It tasted unusual, and not near as salty as the meat he was used to eating, and it took several mouthfuls before he got used to it. The bread was also a little different, and again it took several mouthfuls before he got used to that too. In all of his days he had never been so hungry, and all of the food disappeared in a few minutes.

"More Food!" Luke banged his fist down on the table, startling the other customers. He had never acted like this in his life, having a gentle nature despite his incredibly bad temper. He was very frustrated and felt as though his stomach was a bottomless pit that he would never fill. It eventually took three servings before he finally began to relax.

There was a look of astonishment on the tavern keeper's face, as he had never in all his life seen anyone eat so much. There were a few fat, greedy merchants who frequented his premises, but even they were no match for this man's appetite. Luke on the other hand carried less than an ounce of fat, as he was all muscle, which was something that made the other customers very wary.

Luke beckoned the tavern keeper over, and the man, fearing the worst, obeyed.

"What is the unusual taste in the meat?"

Luke had decided that he liked it, particularly after his third helping. The tavern keeper explained about the spices which arrived via the Arab traders who still used this port. Luke thought that it was strange that they still used this port, as a majority of the vessels here were journeying off to the Holy

Land to fight the Muslims, and yet here they were busily trading with the enemy. He also told Luke about the fruit and silks which also arrived here, and, even though he had devoured three helpings, Luke was eager to see if there was any of this fruit available on the quay.

It did not take long for him to make his way back to the quayside, much to the relief of the tavern keeper and his customers. They were thankful that he had not lost his temper, as they all feared for their lives. Word of this mighty warrior quickly spread, and it was not long before talk of Luke was spreading like *wild fire*.

Luke, on the other hand, only had the one thought in his mind, and that was of yet more food. There was only a limited supply of fruit back home, which was grown locally. He had heard rumours of such things as oranges and lemons as well as olives and dates. These rumors originated from Roman times, and such things disappeared along with them.

He was in luck as there were indeed traders with exotic fruits on the quayside, together with all sorts of other items from far off lands. Spices also interested him, and he decided that after, purchasing some fruit, he would also acquire some spices so that he could spread them on his future rations.

The small crowd around the fruit trader soon parted as Luke approached, still looking fearsome, even though his temper had subsided. He still wanted feeding, and it only took him a few moments to acquire what he was after. Luke then made his way to a quieter part of the quayside, sitting on a raised stone wall by another vessel. This was one of the spice traders whom he planned to do business with as soon as he had finished off his fruit. For the first time in his life Luke tasted an orange. It was delicious and quite unlike anything that he had ever tasted before. The lemon was a little sharp and did not taste nearly as good as the orange, although the dates, figs and olives did go down rather well!

Luke stretched up his massive arms rippling his muscles under his armor as finally he felt full. It may have been an awful journey and one that he did not want to make, but at least he had tasted some of the things that were no more than distant rumours in his native land.

Still deep in thought, Luke relaxed with his full stomach wondering how he was now going to complete his journey. He was still deep in thought when the crowd in front of him parted to reveal a priest wearing white robes. He had a gold cross around his neck and displayed the wealth of the church for all to see. He was in complete contrast to the others, and the cut of his cloth was of a much higher quality than any he had seen so far. The priest approached having been informed of the black knight by the rumours that had been spreading quickly around the port.

"Why do you not wear the Lord's Cross?" The priest asked him.

Luke looked up at him in all his splendour, as the sun glistened off his golden cross.

"Because I choose not to!" Luke replied.

"It is blasphemy for a knight not to wear it!!" The priest exclaimed.

"I command you to wear it!" His usual authority, however had little effect on Luke as he raised himself to his feet, towering above him.

Luke felt the taste of the lemon in his mouth as distain for the priest filled his body.

"In the name of God I command it!"

There was silence as Luke stared at him through his large dark brown eyes while he stood there defiantly.

The priest then pointed to him.

"Seize that man!"

From behind the priest appeared four Knights, all wearing the red cross of the Knights Templars, and as they approached, Luke drew the sword of his grandfather. They charged at him and with a few swings of his sword there was a clang of metal as he sent them sprawling. Luke made sure that he only stunned them, using his fists and large boots to knock them off balance. They were no match for him and as they lay on the ground around the priest. Luke suddenly saw the Holy man who he had seen onboard ship walk from the crowd, cross the stone quayside and walk up the gang plank of the spice trader's ship. He could not believe his eyes and without a doubt in his mind he picked up his belongings and followed him up the gangplank, onto their ship.

What followed was quite a commotion as the knights got to their feet and chased after him. Relations between the Arabs and the Crusaders was fragile at best and, fearing that they were about to be embroiled in a fight, the traders decided to set sail. The gangplank was quickly raised, ropes detached and sails hoisted as their vessel slipped away from its moorings. The knights were only feet away, however they seemed to have no real desire to try and jump onto the trader's ship as it got a little further away. Fortunately, being weighed down by their chainmail and heavy swords, they realised that they would probably end up in the water, much to the relief of the traders.

Once they were safely underway some of the trader's gathered around Luke. It was the first time that they had encountered a knight who refused to where the cross, and such a large and powerful one at that. Everything had happened so quickly that no-one had had time to think, and had acted on instinct. It now appeared that they had a guest, and one who no doubt bring them trouble. There was no way that they would be welcome in Lisbon any more, and the growing power and influence of the Church of Rome meant that once news of this spread, they may well not be welcome in a whole host of other ports too. Taking Luke onboard, it had significantly hampered business, and after a short discussion between themselves in Arabic, they decided that their only course of action would be to sail to their home port and face the wrath of their ruler the Sultan.

Luke on the other hand, was still preoccupied with the Holy man, and his eyes searched the ship for any sign of him, but just as in his previous encounter, there was no sign of him anywhere, and he began to think that maybe he was losing his mind…

Six

It was ironic that the last two visions had each ended with me thinking that I was loosing my mind!

I was now really struggling and everything suddenly got on top of me, and in some ways I felt like a boxer who was on the ropes being pounded by a merciless adversary. I wanted to throw in the proverbial towel, and felt that I no longer had the strength to carry on.

It had been such a blow loosing my beloved father, and in struggling on trying to keep strong for my mother, I had failed to deal with my own grief. I am sure that anyone who has suffered grief knows how difficult it is to deal with. It affects everyone differently and there are five main stages of it;

Denial and isolation - where you instinctively block out what is going on and refuse to deal with the emotions. I was terribly upset at the time and just could not believe that such an incredibly strong man had lost the fight for life, and had been taken away from us.

Anger - I am not a person who loses his temper and, and using the analogy of a bomb, I have an incredibly long fuse which would burn itself out long before I exploded. My anger was with myself, as I felt that if I had learned the art of Reiki which is all about healing people then I should have been able to heal my beloved father. Although he was eighty four years of age and had lived a wonderful life, it had been his time to leave us, even though we desperately wanted him to stay.

Bargaining - I tried my very best to use what I had learnt to change places with him. In my mind I loved him so very much that I would gladly have given my own life to save his. Again this is documented in my book *A Way of being - The Journey to Spiritual Enlightenment.*

Depression - This was the stage that I was at. I had tried everything, and with my illness, experiences with Luke and my failure to deal with my grief I was convinced that I had lost my mind!

Acceptance - I have now reached this point and can celebrate my beloved father's life and achievements, reflect on all the wonderful memories and give thanks that I was so lucky to have had such a wonderful father.

It was like an emotional tsunami breaking over me and I sat on a chair shaking, with tears rolling down my cheeks and asking to be locked away in a padded cell. My mother, who was also struggling, was so worried that she sent for my Reiki Master.

He duly arrived carrying a large purple sheet about half a meter square. These sheets are based on work done by a nineteenth century Serbian inventor *Nikola Tesla*, and are made of aluminium about 2 millimetres thick. Apparently the atoms have been altered so that they are in tune with the basic energy of nature and the universe, and the field of energy that they create can return any damaged cells to their normal vibrational rate. Obviously I was not vibrating correctly!

So there I sat as he stood in front of me with his purple sheet. He had a bushy beard and looked like the seventies Greek singer *Demis Roussos*, wearing an Australian bush hat like *Crocodile Dundee*. He set about waving the purple sheet above my head like *Rolf Harris's wobble board*, chanting a mantra. I just looked at him as a thought manifested in my mind. Looking objectively at the situation, I seemed to be quite sane in comparison to the man standing in front of me. My tears of sadness turned to ones of laughter, and both my wonderful mother and myself began to laugh. The laughter developed into a real belly laugh which seemed to last for quite a while.

My Reiki Master left with a broad smile on his face thinking that he had cured me, whilst my wonderful mother and myself seemed to have had a large weight lifted from our shoulders. I had reached rock bottom but, by letting go of all of the emotions that I had been bottling up for months, I began to feel a whole lot better. That night I had the best sleep that I had had for some considerable time. There were no visions either, which came as a bit of a relief!

Things really began to settle down and we finally began to adjust to life without the great man.

However, my Reiki Master did have another surprise for me...

I was in my bedroom watching a documentary on television, whilst my mother was downstairs watching the soaps. It was something that I had pre-recorded - a *Horizon Special*, on the latest scientific theory of how the universe works. Little did I realise that my own perspective was about to change!

The phone rang and my mother answered it, calling me downstairs before passing the receiver over to me. It was my Reiki master who was extremely excited. He informed me that there was a *U.F.O.* over the house!

I nearly dropped the receiver as I told my mother what he had just said. We looked at each other before looking out of the window, but could not see anything unusual.

There then followed a lengthy pause as I put the receiver down and we went into the lounge, both needing to sit down. The rest of the evening was spent having another one of those 'what have you got yourself involved with' lectures by my mother.

The morning brought a fresh start, and we went shopping as usual. I drove us into town and I treated my mother to a coffee and a large gooey cake. Everything seemed normal until the evening paper arrived. There, splashed all over the front, was my Reiki master with a picture of a space ship hovering above our house. My mother nearly dropped the paper and I had to help her to her chair!

Apparently it was a large black triangular shaped craft with a white light in each corner and one in the centre. My Reiki master , who was a retired *Sergeant Major* in the *Royal Artillery,* described how he had never seen anything like it before. He went on to described how it had appeared in the sky and the direction in which it left. The military and local airports had been contacted, but no unusual activity had been recorded. Suffice to say that we both had a few sleepless nights after that!

It must have been a month or so later when curiosity got the better of me and I began to think more seriously about Luke. Was he really a past life or just a figment of my imagination?

I really needed to know one way or another, as I felt as though it was the one thing holding back my recovery. I did some research and came across something called the *Akashic Records*. Akashic is a Sanskrit word which means sky, space or ether and is described as being a compendium of mystical knowledge encoded in a non-physical plane of existence. The Akashic records are described as containing all knowledge of human experience and the history of the cosmos. This seemed like a good place to start, as the last thing that I wanted was to go and see another hypnotherapist - one past life is enough for anyone to be going on with!

There are those who teach about it, and courses that you can attend where they teach you how to access them. There were none in my locality, and the ones I did find were rather on the expensive side. I did however find one on *eBay* with what they term as a *distant attunement*. This seemed like a bit of a long shot, particularly as you never quite know what you will be getting. After a great great deal of thought, and against my better judgment, I ordered one.

The information came through via the internet and I booked in a day and time for the attunement to take place. Apparently the person sending the attunement has to prepare things for you before sending it. When the allotted time approached, I settled down on the couch closed my eyes and readied myself for whatever was going to happen, with feelings of trepidation. What if it was all a con and nothing happened?

At least it was not that expensive, and I might just have to put it down to experience, having learnt my lesson. Still thinking that I had made a mistake I felt a bright light inside my head. At first I thought that was the start of a headache as I began to feel a little dizzy. I was just starting to convince myself that I was imagining it when I started to feel light headed. It felt very strange, and I must admit, a little exciting. What if it was really working and I had not been conned after all!

Then quite unexpectedly, I saw a vision of a stone building floating in the clouds. It had a large stone arched doorway with a set of large oak doors with black metal hinges. As I approached, the doors opened and I travelled inside. It was a little like a church without pews, and where the font would be was a small wooden table with a large book sitting on it. The book was quite thick and resembled something that you would expect to see in a museum dating from the Middle Ages. The book opened, and I could see the pages moving until they stopped about half way through. This intrigued me and I felt myself studying the strange language written on the thick parchment-like paper as the scene began to change...

―――

Luke stood outside the blacksmith's eager to get on with making his armour, and especially his boots. He found the traditional chainmail and armour worn by knights cumbersome and ineffective, as it slowed him down and restricted his movement. For months now he had been designing his own lightweight version, which involved the use of boiled leather. The initial idea came from the book bindings in his father's library, and the fact that from an early age he had been encouraged to read the books in there.

The Romans had lightweight armor and he had studied it for quite some time. The leather itself was first boiled in water together with oil, wax and fermented animal urine. Although quite pungent, it did cause the leather to harden and become pliable so that the strips could be stitched together. What interested Luke was having the leather strips stitched around small metal plates to form strong lightweight panels that could be bound together with leather straps. This would create a protective skin allowing greater movement and a great deal of protection.

Boots were also items that he found inadequate, and he planned to use a similar construction for them too. There would also have to be arm protectors which would be strapped to his biceps and forearms to act as shields. Luke preferred not to carry a traditional shield and he fought with either both hands on the sword of his grandfather or occasionally also used a second sword. Once the metal strips had been fashioned, it would be up to the leather smith to put everything together.

Luke became impatient as the blacksmith got his furnace up to temperature. Once this was achieved, they spent many hours fashioning his designs.

As I turned the page, the scene changed to one with the leather smith...

Luke was now directing the leather smith as the pungent odor began to change the leather into the hardened strips he was after. It would take several days for all of the panels to be made, and then pieced together, before he could have his first fitting.

I continued to turn the pages as Luke's armour began to take shape. I then moved forward to where he was onboard the spice trader's ship...

It was several days since Luke had ventured onboard, and after the initial shock things had settled down. There was a growing admiration between him and the crew, as they had never encountered a knight who had refused to wear the cross, or indeed someone who was so formidable. The Arab world had been shaken by the Crusades, as the Church of Rome increased its influence, seeking to unify everyone under its control, not to mention to take control of the trade routes, which included the silk and spice roads. It was as much about trade as it was about religion, and neither was of interest to Luke. All he desired was to get to the Holy Land, observe what he could, and then return to his beloved as soon as possible. He had even begun to learn how to speak the Arabs language and learn how to read their script. Apparently they had vast libraries of knowledge and were considerably more advanced than he had realised. It would be ironic if he was sent out to discover all that he could about this new religion and return as a Muslim!

Luke had no intention of taking up any religion, although he did find their holy book fascinating. It was slow going as he struggled to learn to read their script, although the captain was a good teacher. He actually welcomed Luke's presence, and the crew in general were a good deal friendlier than the people he had travelled to Lisbon with. He had a thirst for knowledge and reveled in the tales they told of far off lands and different cultures. This would bode well as their journey would be long and, once they arrived, he would be introduced to the Sultan.

I suddenly began to feel very tired as the vision faded, and I returned to the couch. I must have been unconscious for at least an hour, and, when I was fully aware of my surroundings I opened my eyes. I felt none the wiser, as I still could not decide whether this was all part of my imagination. A hall of records in the sky with a large leather bound book containing all of my past lives - this seemed to me to be another delusion, and I decided that I would leave it there. The last thing that I wanted was to slip back to where I had been, although the thought of my Reiki Master and his *purple wobble board* did bring a smile to my face!

Seven

Time passed, and the very close bond that I shared with my wonderful mother strengthened, as we came to terms with the loss of my beloved father. Things settled down, although there were more strange encounters to come...

I was asked to create a web site by another angel artist friend for someone that she knew who was trying to set up a charity similar to the one I was involved with. I felt that I could not refuse and so agreed to meet her. She duly arrived at our house and was not quite what we expected. She was suffering from *Cerebral Palsy* - a condition which affects the brain causing problems with movement, posture and co-ordination and had a squint, limp and a hump!

From the outset, despite her appearance, she was more than a little *strange* becoming obsessed with me to the point where she was telling all her friends that we were going to get married. Her fantasy also grew into one where we were going to produce a daughter who was going to mate with the son her best friend was going to produce, to bring forth the new messiah!

We only learnt of this later, when we were contacted by my angel-artist friend, who had received a very distressed call from one of her male friends. Apparently, my *admirer* had gone into his shop with her best friend, who happened to be a very large single lady, and when they informed him that he was going to mate with this lady to produce a son, he had taken flight and locked himself in the toilet!

All of this had happened a few days before her final visit, and her extreme behavior was about to take another turn for the worst!

She arrived unexpectedly, and both my mother and myself felt decidedly uncomfortable, and this feeling was not helped by the wild look in her eyes.

Something had to be done, and so I decided to go upstairs to clear my mind. I was going to tell her that I was no longer comfortable with the web site and that maybe she should find someone else.

So, I left her downstairs with my mother whilst I went upstairs to compose myself. I was going to go back downstairs, tell her of my decision, and then ask her to leave.

Unfortunately, I had not anticipated that she would follow me upstairs. I was startled as she appeared behind me, and as I turned round, she suddenly ripped her clothes off and as I stood there in a state of shock, launched herself at me, knocking me onto my bed before diving on top of me!

I felt a very sharp pain in my back as I tore a muscle, but still managed to push her off and to get her downstairs and out through the front door!

Both my mother and I were deeply shocked and I ceased my involvement in the project and she was banned from our home. There then followed a period of *stalking* when our lives were turned upside down. The culmination of this was when my mother started to have nightmares. she dreamed that she was tied to a chair in a damp cellar with water running down the walls, then thrown down some stone steps by my *admirer,* who was laughing like a witch!

My mother awoke in quite a state and, as she got out of bed and made her way towards the bathroom, there standing guard in the doorway she saw Luke. For some reason I awoke and my mother described him exactly as I saw him. He was massive with black boiled leather armour, dark collar-length wavy hair, and dark beard. He was standing there with his hands on the hilt of an enormous sword which my mother said was almost as tall as her. It was quite a conversation, and we both began to doubt our sanity!

Fortunately, after a few phone calls, my *admirer's* family were contacted and she received the help that she needed. My mother also received some counseling and we managed to put the whole experience behind us.

We did, however, have another bizarre experience involving a former Franciscan Monk. He contacted me via my angel-artist friend and asked me whether I would help him arrange a course, as he lived out of the area. I agreed, feeling that it would do no harm, after all what could possibly go wrong?

He arrived and was very sociable and got on well with my wonderful mother. We did our best to help and that night he stayed in our spare room. About three o'clock in the morning my mother awoke and decided to go to the bathroom, as she opened her bedroom door, there was the monk, naked as the day he was born crossing the landing!

My mother said that he looked all pink and scrubbed like a cherub!

So, after a stalker with a squint, limp and a hump we now had our very own streaking monk to deal with!

With this in mind, maybe the encounters with Luke were not so strange after all!

Luke seemed to take a bit of a back seat for the next few months as both my wonderful mother and myself tried to keep a very low profile. My mother put her foot down and I agreed to distance myself from all the *spiritual stuff*, and I bought myself an electronic drum kit. It was great as I could play it with headphones on and not disturb anyone. Getting back into music was something which she felt would do me good, and although I struggled to play it as I was still not back to good health, at least I could not get myself into any more trouble!

The only thing that I missed was my weekly aqua detox treatment, which I had been having at the therapy centre. So I purchased a machine myself. It is a bit controversial as you place your feet in a bowl of saline water and a metallic coil is then placed in the bowl. The basic idea is that the coil removes toxins through your feet and cleanses the system. There are many claims and counter claims about the machine. Some people are convinced that it works, whilst others claim that it is a fraud. I was one of those that thought that it offered some real benefits, so when it arrived by post, I set it up in the living room.

I had just placed my feet in the warm water and switched on the timer when the door bell rang. My mother had decided that she needed an interest and so had made enquiries about the *Women's Institute*. Two very posh ladies entered and were guided into the living room. I greeted them briefly explaining about the machine whilst my mother put the kettle on, returning with a tray and some cakes.

I completely forgot that I had undone my trouser button to get more comfortable, and rolled my trouser legs up before placing my feet in the warm water. My mind was drifting and the ladies engaged in polite conversation until the buzzer sounded signalling the end of the aqua detox session. I removed my feet from the bowl, drying them on my towel as the ladies glanced at me. I pretended to take no notice as I stood up, disconnected the cable and lifted up the bowl ready to take it into the kitchen to empty down the sink. I had the feeling that they thought I was a little *strange*, and this feeling was confirmed as I crossed the room and my trousers began to slip. There I was standing in front of them with the bowl of water in my hands, my trousers down around my ankles wearing nothing but a T shirt and my boxer shorts - both it has to be said presents from my mother. There was a look of horror on their faces, as there, printed on the material was a picture of a rhinoceros with the words *horny beast* written underneath!

Suffice to say that they suddenly remembered that they had a prior engagement and hurriedly left!

My mother never did get an invite to joint the *Women's Institute!*

Eight

Unfortunately, my wonder mother's health began to deteriorate, and I sought the advice of a very kind lady who I used to work alongside at the therapy centre. She was very gifted and said that she would pop in to see her on her way home. The doorbell rang and as we went to greet her, my mother asked me if she was at all *weird*, thinking of our previous encounters. I assured her that she was quite normal, and when we opened the door we were met with a large lady holding a clump of sage and a lighter. We both looked at each other as she exclaimed. "I am so sorry, I can't come in as I have got to go and clear a house which is full of ghosts, can I call in tomorrow?"

She did come to see us, and although she seemed to have a few *strange ideas* was very nice and quite helpful. She encouraged my mother to go to the doctors, which she did. He was of little use and, when my mother stated that she was having difficulty eating he blamed the dentist for a recent filling. For some reason my mother had faith in him, which was more than I did as he was the one who administered the antibiotics that caused all of my health problems!

I was very worried and that evening I had a very restless sleep, as my mind was searching for answers. However, I was not the only one to be doing this…

The Sultan was a very cultured man and one who possessed great wisdom having studied in Persia and he had collated his own library within his palace. He had copies of many of the ancient texts translated into Arabic, with everything from Greek philosophers to those of India and China. There were also books on science and mathematics and he used the wealth gained from his trade routes in a very positive way. He was intrigued when he heard of

Luke, the black knight who refused to wear the cross, and summoned him to his palace.

Luke bowed before the Sultan showing him respect, and the Sultan returned the compliment bowing back. He had brilliant blue eyes and typically Arabic hooked nose and olive skin. Luke also had an olive skin due to the sunlight and with his dark hair and beard, could almost have passed for an Arab himself. He had learned such a lot on his voyage and could not only speak Arabic but, more importantly, read it too.

Luke was very fortunate, as it was deemed a great honour to meet the Sultan, and he was the only Knight to have ever met him off the battle field. His influence extended far and wide and although a devout Muslim, he was open to hear and read about many things. One of the main beliefs of Islam is that Muslims should help those in need.

Luke was certainly in need, as it seemed to him that he had upset the entire Christian world, or at least any Christian he had encountered so far. Looking at the Sultan he wondered whether he would be forced to become a Muslim?

To his amazement, the Sultan guided him to a chair, and, as both men sat down, the Sultan politely asked him to relay the events that had brought him to these lands. It was quite a tale, and one which Luke gladly shared. There was something almost magical about the Sultan, who was the most charismatic man that he had ever met. He just sat there occasionally nodding his head as Luke relayed his story. It was as though he was in some ways gaining knowledge of the far off land that had produced the vast army which had taken control of the Holy Land. He was particularly interested in why Luke had not taken up the cross, realising that not everyone from this far off land had desires of conquest.

It was some time later that the Sultan put the flat of his left hand up, signalling Luke to finish, whilst he held his chin with his right hand as he considered the situation. After a few moments of deep thought, the Sultan offered Luke the use of his library and quarters for as long as he wished to stay, and asked for nothing in return. Luke was shocked at his kindness and generosity. He had never met such an educated man before, who not once mentioned his own faith, let alone forcing him to become a convert.

Luke gladly accepted and as both men rose to their feet, he nodded respectfully to the Sultan who bowed back. The Sultan then signalled to one of his staff informing him of his decision, and Luke was led off towards his new quarters. This posed quite a question in his mind. Why did his supposed enemy offer him so much, and yet the new religion of his homeland wanted to take so much?

Luke spent most of the next month within the walls of the Sultan's library seeking answers, until he received a message form the Sultan. There was a caravan due to depart for Jerusalem and would he like to be part of it?

This was an opportunity too good to refuse, and he gladly accepted. The Sultan was indeed a wise man for his sister would be travelling with the caravan, and he knew that having the mighty black Knight within it would offer her greater protection.

Luke was allocated a horse - the Sultan was quite a horseman, and Pasha was one of his finest, being a large white thoroughbred stallion that was highly intelligent, although still only partially broken in. He was stubborn and bad tempered, with a mind of his own - much like Luke!

Their eyes met for the first time as they weighed each other up, much as boxers do before a bout. Neither gave an inch as they stared each other out. Luke moved slowly towards Pasha as he held his ground, standing proudly with his ears erect and his head held high. Luke was only a few feet away now but Pasha did not flinch. There was no way he was going to allow anyone to ride him, and if they tried to mount, then he was going to throw them off, just like he had done with everyone else.

The Sultan looked on as Luke stood only a few inches away, slowly raising his right hand. Pasha looked on, ready to rear himself, as Luke gently rubbed the knuckle of his index finger on the side of Pasha's cheek. He still did not flinch as Luke moved his hand slowly towards the horses nose, gently rubbing the short bristly hair above his nostrils. Luke then bent forwards gently blowing into Pasha's nostrils, still gently caressing him. The Sultan looked on as Pasha placed his head on Luke's right shoulder, as Luke gently stroked him beneath his right ear.

There was something almost magical about what was going on, and the Sultan smiled broadly as the two of them continued to bond. He had never seen anything quite like it as Luke continued to caress Pasha. He was now gently rubbing him between the ears, and as Pasha bent down, he whispered something in his ear. It was as if Pasha could understand every word as he stood, whilst Luke moved round to his side, still caressing him.

To the Sultan's amazement, Luke gently mounted him, still rubbing the side of his neck. Pasha still failed to flinch, and instead began to walk slowly forwards as if under some sort of spell. Everyone else who had tried to mount Pasha had been thrown straight off, and the Sultan had grown impatient with him. With all of his years' experience with horses he had never seen anything quite like it!

He allowed them a few more days to get better acquainted before assembling the caravan. It was going to be a long journey, but a necessary one. It was important to keep the dialogue going, as there were many on each side who wished to go to war. The Sultan was a man of peace, along with King Baldwin IV and between them, and others of like mind, they had managed to hold the truce. The journey would give Luke time to think, as there were still many unanswered questions in his mind.

The Sultan's library was vast and it would have taken any scholar several lifetimes to read all of the contents, and even with the help of the keeper of books, Luke had only managed to scratch the surface. His Arabic, although improving, was still quite weak and there still many phrases that he had to learn. The keeper had been very helpful, and Luke had learned much, although it had to be said that he was none the wiser. Not only were there books on the new religion, but also on the Sultan's faith, and other faiths from India and beyond.

It just seemed as though the more he read the new religion's book, the more uncomfortable he had became with it. There were accounts of whole cities being destroyed, not to mention the flood which also took so many lives, all caused by their god. Some ancient texts had been translated from Greek, others from Roman, and yet nowhere could he find the peace that he sought. It all just seemed far to complicated and based on a philosophy of power and control. All he knew was that people who wore the cross seldom acted with compassion and understanding, and maybe he would find the answers he sought only when they reached Jerusalem.

The Sultan presented his sister to him, and Luke bowed respectfully. She wore a black veil over most of her face, with only her deep brown hypnotic eyes showing, which portrayed many hidden gifts. He recognised the knowing in her eyes, the same in those of his own secret love, and he guessed that she was also knowledgeable in the healing arts. There were also twenty of the Sultan's men who were going to accompany them, along with two horses laden with supplies.

It would be a long hot ride, particularly for someone wearing body armour, and a journey across the desert was the last thing that Luke envisioned when he designed it. There was no way that he would be travelling without it, however, he loosened off its protective layers as best as he could. Over the top he wore a long white cloak to protect him from the sun, and a turban around his head. The Sultan smiled to himself at the sight of the knight who refused to wear the cross about to embark on a journey to the Holy Land dressed as an Arab!

Nine

Luke was not the only one who was about to embark on a hazardous journey, as about a month later I was asked to do a commission. Initially it seemed quite straightforward, and when it was finished, I decided to deliver it in person, as opposed to sending it via courier. It was only in South Warrington, which was not that far away. I took my mother along with me, to give her a bit of a break. She always liked meeting new people, and considering we had been keeping a low profile, I thought that it would do us both good. On the surface everything seemed fine, but little did I realise that underneath there lay a very devious plan!

Shortly afterwards my wonderful mother became seriously ill and the lady who had commissioned the picture made several visits, apparently being concerned about the situation. The doctor was still blaming the dentist, when we knew that there was something seriously amiss. One morning I awoke to find my mother's skin had turned yellow, and when I took her to see the doctor, she emerged with the news that she a large cancerous tumour in her liver and was going to die!

The doctor made an appointment with a specialist, who we managed to see a few days later. He was shocked that there had been no tests and he dismissed the doctor's diagnosis, suggesting that she went to hospital for some tests before a proper diagnosis could be made.

The lady who I had done the commission for offered to move in with us to help me care for my mother. Initially I was very grateful for as a man there is only so much that you can do for your mother. My mother's eldest brother also decided to move in, and he took over all of my mother's affairs brushing me aside. All I was concerned about was my mother, and making her as comfortable as possible. If she did come out of hospital then she would need specialist care, which would be expensive. Money was the last thing on my mind, but sadly not on her brother's!

He refused to grant me access to any paperwork, and I had no knowledge of whether any bills had been paid, or if it was going to be possible to pay for specialist care. I was very upset only wanting the very best for my mother, but her brother held on tightly to her purse strings!

What followed was a traumatic six weeks which resulted in my wonderful mother being taken from me by pancreatic cancer, I was absolutely devastated.

I was now alone in the world and very vulnerable and before I knew what was happening I found myself in a strange town sharing a house with the person who I believed had been my saviour. She formed an alliance with my mother's eldest brother and they tried, but failed, to force me to hand over all of my late mother's estate! (This again is part of my book *A Way of Being - The Journey to Spiritual Enlightenment*)

I did feel Luke's presence which, along with my beloved father's seemed to be there for me. I could just sense that they were there, and received several *signs*, which was just as well, as the person who I thought was my saviour did everything to destroy me.

They say that it is always darkest before the dawn, and my light came in the form of my beloved soul mate Catherine. She arrived like an angel and made the sun shine in my life again. It had been several years since I had encountered Luke, and it was now time for him to make another appearance…

———

The Temple Mount loomed on its elevated plateau, looking out towards the walls of the ancient city, with its golden dome glistening in the bright sunlight.

Amongst all the different faiths it stood there connecting them together, as it was a revered site to Christians, Jews, and Muslims alike. Even to the earlier pagans it was sacred, and maybe this is where Luke would find the answers to the questions posed on his long journey.

Now it was the *Royal Palace* and the headquarters of the *Knights Templar*, and was not going to be the most welcoming of places for a knight who refused to wear the cross, and the Muslim sister of a powerful Sultan.

The king Baldwin IV ruled the land, even though he suffered from leprosy and despite his illness had proved to be a great man. Under his rule there was a truce of sorts, which could be described as fragile at best. It was, however, just enough to enable Muslims access to the city, although they were not allowed to live within its walls.

The gates to the city were open, but they were guarded by some surly looking knights and accompanying foot soldiers. This less than welcoming sight greeted them as they neared the outer walls.

It took quite a lot of persuasion for Luke and the Sultan's sister to be allowed through, although the rest of the party were forced to stay outside the city. There was access to water and a little food though, which was at least something.

The knights escorted them through the gates, and would stay with them all the way to the Royal Palace. There was an air of mistrust, and it was apparent that the fragile peace was even more delicate than they had been led to believe.

Luke began to wonder if they would be allowed inside the Royal Palace, and maybe it was the fact that the Sultan's envoy was a woman, and his sister at that, that was going to make it possible at all. One of the knights had gone on ahead to inform the King of their presence, and it was touch and go as to whether he would be well enough to see them.

Their whole mission hung in the balance as they caught sight of the new arches of the central bays of the main façade, recently installed by the Templars. There were yet more knights guarding them as their escorts took them to within a few feet of the Royal Palace.

Fortune was on their side, and they were granted access to the Palace. The king was having one of his better days, and the Sultan was indeed a wise man sending his sister as an envoy.

They were asked to dismount and their horses were led away to be watered whilst they were ushered inside. Again there seemed to be an air of mistrust and the knights were clearly unhappy with the situation. They respected the King and followed his orders, which Luke felt was the only thing stopping them from being attacked.

He now had the opportunity to see at first hand what it was that marked this place out as being so special to the Christians, Muslims and Jews alike. Being asked to be the Sultan's sister's protector was a master stroke, as not only being one of the most powerful warriors he had ever seen, but being of the same creed as the King, not of the same faith singled Luke out from other men. Luke could feel the Sultan's guiding hand, although he was not oblivious to the fact that it suited the Sultan to use him in such a manner. Word had reached the King of this black knight who refused to wear the cross he was intrigued as to why he was here, and his reasons for refusing to dedicate himself to the new religion.

The recently founded *Knights Templars* had started excavating the Temple Mount immediately following their arrival at the time of the first crusade. There had been a strong rumour that although the Romans destroyed the original temple of Solomon long ago, there were valuable treasures still buried beneath the ruins.

The *Al Aqsa Mosque* as the Muslims called the Palace, had been built on the site many years later. Beneath lay tunnels known as Solomon's stables, which the Templar's had made use of. There were also rumours of riches which had been discovered, which only added to the mysteries.

In Luke's mind everything about this new religion pointed to the gathering of wealth and control over the people. Luke was a considerably wealthy man by any measure, although he cared nothing for it. It had brought him no happiness, as all he sought was peace, and the love of the one he been forced to leave behind. He also felt that, in a similar way the riches of the Sultan had not brought him much happiness either. Although he was a kind and just ruler, Luke could sense the immense responsibility he felt resting on his shoulders. His people looked up to him, and his only escape was to immerse himself in his library. That was one thing that they both shared - a thirst for knowledge. There was a word which prevented both of them from pursuing their wishes fully, and that was *duty*.

According to the texts which he had read, the Mount of Olives was where Jesus made his ascension, and the prophet *Muhammad* had a vision of his own ascension. There was even a sacred stone called the *Sela foundation stone*, where Muhammad rested on his spiritual journey.

This place was indeed steeped in history, and if it was so special to so many, then it begged the question why everyone should not share it, instead of fighting for control over it? Control was something which seemed to be in abundance and freedom was nothing more than a distant aspiration.

They were both led through a series of rooms before they entered the King's chambers. Luke was asked to surrender his sword, which was something that he had only ever done once before, and that was for the Sultan. He did however, have several other blades secretly hidden within his armour! The knights looked uneasy as he pulled the sword of his grandfather from behind his back. It was larger than the normal crusader swords, and the look he gave them was enough for them to realise that their own lives were more at risk than the King's!

The King lay on a bed being attended to by his sister Isabella. They were very close and he relied on her, as well as several others who helped him with his condition. He had fresh bandages on his hands and his face was covered by a mask. His condition was laying waste to his body, although his mind was still very active.

He beckoned them closer, wanting to get a good look at the black knight who had proved to be quite an enigma since his appearance in the *Promised Land*. The King seemed to be just as interested in him as the Sultan, and so he gave the same explanation as he had done to him.

The King understood and respected his words, understanding that it was one thing to follow blindly what you have been told, and quite another to find out things for yourself. If it was faith that he was after, then this could not be a better place to find it. The King then gestured to one of his servants who placed a neatly bound package on the bed, before unwrapping it. The wrappings revealed an ornate sword with crystals embedded in the hilt. They started off with red, and the rainbow continued until it reached the top where there was a large clear stone. The King explained that it had been excavated from under the Palace, literally drawn out of the stone, and was to be presented to the Sultan as a gift.

Luke took the sword, assuring him that he would present it to the Sultan.

The King then offered Luke use of his private chapel, so that he may seek the answers to the many questions that he had come here with. Luke bowed before the King, and was then led away through a side room. He was shocked, as there kneeling at the alter was the holy man!

Luke knelt beside him, placing the sword between his hands as he knelt. He presumed it was the place where those seeking absolution went after battle. To him it was quite profound, as he himself always asked for forgiveness whenever he had been forced into a similar situation. Luke was still seeking peace, although from what he had already witnessed there seemed to be a very slim chance of success. So far all he had witnessed was a zealous craving to destroy all those who did not hold a particular view. The King had managed to gain a peace of sorts although there were many knights who sort battle with the Muslims, and were determined to undermine him. It had taken great skill to keep the fragile peace alive.

Luke closed his eyes in this most holy of places, seeking a connection with whatever energies made it so holy. Emptying his mind, he allowed whatever thoughts were meant to be drift into his mind. Everywhere was so quiet, in contrast to the hustle and bustle of life outside, as he recounted the prayer that had been written in the holy book he carried with him.

Our heavenly Father, hallowed is your name.
Your Kingdom is come. Your will is done,
As in heaven so also on earth.
Give us the bread for our daily need.
And leave us serene,
just as we also allowed others serenity.
And do not pass us through trial,
except separate us from the evil one.
For yours is the Kingdom,
the Power and the Glory
To the end of the universe, of all the universes,

Amen!

The silence was almost defining as he knelt there in contemplation seeking answers to the many questions he had about the new ways. Nothing seemed to be happening as he sought a sign, something that would confirm why so many people had such great faith, had travelled from so far and wide, and were prepared to lay down their lives in the endless battles that had scarred this land for centuries. It seemed to him that it was all about persecution, and that the original message of peace, love and harmony had been lost a very long time ago. Images of all that he had already seen came flooding into his mind, causing a shiver to roll down his spine. It was not what he had expected, although from the outset he had been very strongly opposed to the whole journey. There were some who were genuinely striving for peace, although they were in the minority. Peace was something that he also strived for, and this longing in his heart began to overwhelm him.

Luke was so immersed in his thoughts that he failed to notice a small band of knights creep into the chapel. They approached him silently, drawing their swords as they began to surround him. Luke gently opened his eyes as the caught their reflection on the sword. He could see five men standing around him and he instinctively knew that they were not here for prayer. The nearest one raised his sword between his two hands above his head, and just as he brought it down towards him. Luke, rolled to one side plunging the ornate sword into the knights chest. The man fell as the others advanced. Luke skilfully swung the sword, there was a clang of metal as it collided with the knights sword. He was now filled with rage as he began to attack, wielding the sword skilfully. A blow bounced off his shoulder armour, which only increased his raging temper as another knight was dispatched, followed by another two. There was only one left, and Luke roared like a lion, sending him crashing to the floor with one mighty blow.

Another knight entered the room, but this one was not like the others. He had been sent by the King to find out what all of the commotion was about.

The five knights had betrayed the King and were after the sword, as they felt that it should not be given to a Muslim.

Ten

Luke and the Sultan's sister left the Palace under the escort of the King's most trusted knights. Their horses had been prepared for them and they were soon at the city gates. The rest of the caravan was waiting for them, and everyone was keen to get away as soon as they could.

It must have been about three hours later, when they were in open desert that they saw what appeared to be a patrol of knights approaching from behind them. Luke had an uneasy feeling about them and the caravan closed up into a defensive formation around the Sultan's sister. He kept an eye on the knights as they approached, and when they were relatively close, they drew swords and charged.

Luke turned to face them, drawing the sword of his grandfather and also the ceremonial sword that the king had asked him to present to the Sultan. There was a clang of metal as Luke dispatched the first of the knights quickly followed by a second. The majority of them bypassed him, however, heading straight for the caravan. Several members of the Sultan's sister's escort fell to the ground as a might battle ensued. Luke had two knights around him as he thrust and parried until they were dispatched too.

He could see that the caravan in disarray and that the knights had already taken out a majority of them, suffering several losses of their own. He gently nudged Pasha, who shot forward as he engaged the remaining knights. He was considerably outnumbered, and anger raged through his veins. He had lost his temper many times, but now he was considerably angrier than he had ever been before. His rage increased his already considerable strength and he swung the swords with his legendary expertise sending more of the knights to the ground. Amazingly, they seemed to have little to offer against his superior size and strength and their number was dwindling fast, until one of them landed a blow on his left shoulder. Luke felt a sheering pain as he swung round almost cutting the offending knight in two. He was now running on adrenalin as he circled the Sultan's daughter.

He let out a mighty roar as he dispatched another knight, then another two. The remaining knights had never experienced anyone who could fight like this, and as they had already lost so many of their number, decided to withdraw to save themselves from a similar fate. Luke roared again like a lion as they sped off.

Fortunately, the Sultan's sister was unharmed, although they had lost the rest of the caravan, apart from the supply horses. They were both very thankful for that, as the hot sun shone down and without water they would not be able to make it back. It would be nightfall in only a few hours and they needed to find somewhere to rest the horses.

Luke dismounted and felt a sharp pain I his arm. There was also some blood, although the wound did not seem serious. He checked for survivors, but unfortunately there were none, so he tethered the horses in a line, before remounting. Looking around, he scanned the horizon just in case the knights had regrouped and were going to attack again.

Luke was in pain and held his injured arm as they set of in search of somewhere to spend the night. Without their guide it was going to be difficult to find their way back, although the Sultan's sister knew the terrain having already made the journey several times. She managed to guide them to a watering hole which they had used on their way to the Holy City, and it was with much relief that they spotted in the distance the trees which marked it out from the endless sand.

It still took them an hour or so to reach it, and they were both relieved when they finally stopped. Luke dismounted guiding Pasha and other horses towards the refreshing water. He then returned for the Sultan's sister, helping her off her horse, which he then led to the water. She helped to unload the supply horses, and then they both sat down against a tree, grabbing their drinking vessels.

She gently removed her veil, and he could see her face for the first time. Her skin was smooth and quite fair for an Arab, and she had a healthy red glow in her cheeks. Her dark eyes stared at him more out of curiosity than anything else.

She did not really know quite what to make of him, as he was so different to anyone she had ever encountered before. It was as though there were two people inside him. One was kind and gentle, and loved to read books, whilst the other had a raging temper that struck fear into the very soul.

Without that temper she doubted whether she would be sitting there, and yet she had no fear of him. He was very respectful and showed her great courtesy, and had risked his own life to save hers. Her brother had briefed her on his story and she could feel the anguish he felt inside. She could also see that he was in pain, and that his wound needed attention.

For Luke's part he was equally bemused, for there sat a beautiful educated Arabic woman who was more ladylike than anyone he had ever met before. He had been led to believe that her people were inferior by the arrogance of most of his own so called people. From his experience, they were much better educated, and their academic achievements rivalled those of *Ancient Greece* and *Rome*. With her fair skin she could have passed as a *European*, and with his darkened skin he could have passed as an *Arab*. There really did not seem to be any real difference between the races, only cultural and religious doctrine. It was ironic that he himself had suffered at the hands of his own people and yet received kindness only from his so called enemies. He remembered the story of the *Good Samaritan*, and Luke smiled to himself. She caught him smiling and could sense what he was thinking.

The Sultan's sister pointed to his arm saying something to him in Arabic, and as he looked down he could see the blood stain on his white cloak. Out of one of the bags the supply horses had been carrying, she pulled a bundle of medicines. Luke watched as she gently unwrapped them, noticing that they were not that dissimilar to the ones his own secret love had used on many occasions.

She pointed to his arm, and he raised himself up, removing his blood stained cloak, releasing the leather straps that held his upper body armour in place. It had largely protected him from the heavy blow, although it was not strong enough to prevent the injury he had received. His upper arm and shoulder were badly bruised, and there was a nasty gash where the leather had been pierced.

She helped him off with his armour, and her eyes widened as she saw his muscular torso. He was a lot larger and far more powerful than anyone she had treated before. She moistened some white linen with water from their drinking vessel and gently dabbed his open wound. It did not appear to be deep and would heal in a few days. He grimaced as she spread some healing herbs onto it, and she smiled in the knowledge that beneath his powerful and threatening exterior, he was really a soft and gentle man. They may have been quite different on the outside, and yet they were very similar on the inside. She also longed for peace and had grown weary of the constant wars that erupted over these lands. It all seemed pointless vying for control over this desert land. Both sides wanted the same thing, which was equally as important to all concerned. If it was important, why were they destroying the very thing that they held so dear. Surely by sharing it everyone would be happy. They looked at each other, and without saying a word they understood what each other was thinking.

Luke grimaced again, feeling the stinging pain of the flesh wound. Left untreated it would become septic and he knew that if that happened, he could develop a fever and possibly die. That was what had happened to his father, whose life had been spared by the actions of his own medicine woman. He was very grateful, and looked on admiringly as she bandaged it expertly.

When she had finished, he lay back against the tree and closed his eyes for a moment. It had been another extraordinary day, and one filled with mystery. Apart from the inevitable questions about the whole scenario being played out in these lands, not to mention the questions he still had about the new religion, he was still perplexed about the holy man. Today was the third time that he had seen him, and it seemed as though he was guiding him on his quest. Sometimes he spoke, whilst at others he was just there pointing the way. Whenever he had approached anyone to enquire as to whether they had also seen him, no one else ever had.

In the Sultan's library he had come across something that the Arabs referred to as a *Jinn*. In their past before their prophet Muhammad, they believed in these supernatural spirits who occupied a parallel world to mankind. In some respect they were similar to *angels*, perhaps the holy man was some sort of a *guardian angel*. With this thought in his mind he drifted off to sleep.

Luke awoke with a start, it was daylight and he had slept all night. The Sultan's sister already had the horses prepared and was eager to get under way sensing that the knights would return. He had the same feeling, and after taking a long drink, and refilling the vessel that contained the water, mounted Pasha and they got under way.

The next few days were spent travelling from one water hole to another, and in the evenings they would exchange stories and talk of many things. She was equally as intelligent as her brother and had also spent many hours in his library. Contrary to misconceptions, women were treated with a lot more respect than rumour had dictated. Whether all women were allowed access to such learning, Luke did not really know, but the Sultan was an exceptional man, and in some ways he relied on his sister, as did King Baldwin IV.

It was with great relief that the outskirts of the Sultan's city reached out to greet them, and they realised that they had made it to safety. It had been a real struggle, particularly for Luke who was still carrying his injury. He still longed for peace, and although he had fought many battles he realised that peace was something that was going to elude him. The whole world seemed to be at war and despite so many religions all preaching peace, none of them seemed to practice it. All he wanted was a place to rest and somewhere that he could escape this constant warring.

His wish was about to be granted, as up ahead there seemed to be something resembling a monastery. Of all things, it was a Christian mission, and something quite unexpected. Luke had heard rumours that many of the soldiers from his native land who lived further south, had fled following the war lord who had swept to power further south. Apparently they were now mercenaries and had established themselves within the empire. The world was certainly a very mixed up place!

The dull grey stone walls of the monastery swept up from the hilltop reflecting its barren and austere nature, and even the birds fell silent as they approached on horseback. It was going to be a strange choice for sanctuary for a none believer and a Muslim woman.

The rough track led them up through the trees towards the outer wall, past the remnants of an old farmhouse. It had long been abandoned, partially destroyed in one of the many battles which had plagued this land for years.

Luke banged on the door to be met by a nun, which again was quite unexpected. She was from Briton, and briefly left them while she went in search of the mother superior. He had requested sanctuary, and that they take care of Sultan's sister while he recuperated. Luke had developed a fever despite of the herbs that had been placed on his wound, and felt that he needed time to recuperate. There were still many dangers to face before they reached the Sultan's palace, and he felt that he could not offer the level of protection he would normally provide. She accepted his decision realising that he was right. She had done her best to treat him, replacing his bandages and treating his wound every night. Under normal circumstances it would not have been advisable to travel with such a wound, but these were far from normal.

For three days Luke lay on a simple wooden bed, vowing never to have anything to do with Knights, battle or religion ever again. He felt the frustration of everything as his fever made his mind race. Everything was swirling around in his head and he missed his secret love. Every night when they had made camp, he had looked into the flames thinking of her. It felt like another lifetime, and he began to wonder whether there was indeed such a thing.

He was suddenly brought back to reality by the sound of screams coming from inside the monastery. At first he thought that he was dreaming, but his head felt clear as the fever had passed. Luke quickly slipped on his boots and the main part of his body armour over his head, instinctively grabbing the swords and dashing out into the corridor. Up ahead in the main dining room he could see a band of marauding knights, who he suspected had followed them here. They must have regrouped and had been joined by others. He was concerned about the Sultan's sister and incensed that he had been disturbed from his slumberings.

Luke roared like a lion, just as he had done when he faced them in the desert, and charged at them with the sword of his grandfather raised high above his head. He was now back to full strength and able to wield it with his usual ferocity. There was carnage in the main dining room as he vented all of his considerable frustration upon them. It was a terrible sight which even shocked Luke. When he had finished and they were no more left standing, he vowed then and there never to fight again.

It was all too much for him and he sank to the ground in floods of tears. The Sultan's sister appeared, wrapping her arms around him like a mother would do to a child. He had saved them all, and now he needed saving from himself!

His temper had died along with the knights, and for the first time he felt peace within himself.

Eleven

Luke waited outside the large ornate door of the Sultan's private chambers. Inside was his sister, briefing him on the events that had transpired since they had left the safety of his palace. It was quite a story, and one which she would not have been telling if it were not for Luke. He was now a changed man having gained the answers to the many questions he had been seeking.

No matter what you believe or how you believe it there is only one definition of *God* that is true, and that is *love*. He now understood that the real God is love, and that life is all about giving and receiving this love unconditionally, and to do this you must love yourself, as well as your fellow man.

This is the message that the holy books, and those who preached from them, should be portraying. These times were so full of conflict that there was little room for love, and he now understood why both the Sultan and King Baldwin IV were working so hard to give it room to grow. From what he had experienced, he could see that most of the people were not ready for this yet, and he hoped that in years to come, the time would be right for it to flourish.

With this thought in mind he entered the Sultan's chambers, bowing before him. The Sultan bowed back as Luke presented the sword of the stone to him as requested by the King.

The Sultan could see in his eyes that he was a changed man, and offered his gratitude for delivering his sister safely back to him. He then offered Luke a place in his library where he could continue to study. This was something that he desperately wanted to accept, but he was bound by duty to his father to return home.

Luke respectfully declined, although it was what he really wanted, that and to be reunited with his secret love. The Sultan was already one step ahead of him, and signalled one of his staff, who opened an adjoining door. From behind its ornate woodcarvings came forth a woman dressed in a long flowing scarlet cloak, with her head covered by a hood. Luke looked a little bemused, as she stood before him, and was deeply shocked when she pulled it back to reveal her face. There standing before him was a beautiful tall slim woman with hazel eyes containing golden specks and flowing blonde hair. He felt rooted to the spot and was deeply in shock, for there stood the one he loved!

They embraced as his heart was filled with joy, and the Sultan smiled broadly, before leaving the room. There were so many questions that Luke had in his mind as he wondered why she had left their homeland, and how she had managed to find him. It was not the happiest of answers that he received when she explained what had transpired.

A few days after he had left, news reached the king of a large army approaching from the south. Rumours of this had already reached him, and what he had been fearing was now here. It was the same army that had taken control of the most of the lands that stretched all the way to the south coast of these islands.

For many years great struggles had taken place, and the crown had passed through several hands as different kings fought for control. Eventually one did succeed, and it was his army that was now attempting to unite the whole of these islands. In his heart he knew that they would be too strong for his own army and that it would be inevitable that his own kingdom would fall. He had summoned her to his chambers, explaining the situation, and why he had sent Luke away. He knew that his son would have fought to the death to save his kingdom, as he did not wish him to die. She had made her way to the coast and boarded a ship just before the army arrived. Others had also managed to flee, and she had received news from them shortly after she arrived in Lisbon.

The battle had been fierce and the King had held out for many days. The loss of life was great and eventually the castle walls had been breached. From all accounts the King had fought very bravely until finally being overwhelmed as the castle was laid to ruin.

Luke put his head in his hands, filled with regret, wishing that he had disobeyed his father and not ventured on his journey. He would have fought alongside his father and maybe there was a chance that together they would have been victorious. If he had have done this however, he would not have found the answer to his questions, and would have had to go through many more lifetimes until he received it…

Twelve

That was the last experience that I had with Luke, and, as far as I know he did remain with his love, and eventually became the *Keeper of Books* in the library of the Sultan.

It is extraordinary to think that so much can happen in such a relatively short space of time, although time is not really what we think it is. In fact, life itself is not really what we think it is either!

Our concept of life has changed over time, as has the concept of *God/Divine* or whatever else it is described as being. It can best be described as *all-knowing*. It experiences itself through us by our own experiences. We are all connected, and together with everything in creation, we form one large consciousness. This consciousness forms what is referred to as a *cosmic grid* or *web*, and our thoughts and experiences are constantly transforming it. When every possible outcome has been experienced, then it will only exist as pure thought. In other words all matter will cease to exist and it will go back to a state of pure consciousness. When there is a desire to experience again, thought will explode into matter in a *big bang*, and the whole process will start all over again.

At the centre of this cosmic grid there is a state referred to as *Nirvana*. In this state there is only bliss. However, it is not possible to remain there for very long, as there has to be an equal and opposite component to show what this state of being really is. You have to experience what is not bliss to know what bliss really is.

The whole concept of the soul is quite an extraordinary one too. There is actually only the one soul, one being, and one essence dividing itself into every living thing in the universe - the *all that is,* which comprises of all sentient beings. This one soul is constantly reforming and reshaping itself, and this process may even be called the *reformation*. It could also be said that we are all divine in formation, and what we all experience is *Divine Information*!

This one soul reforms itself into smaller and smaller parts of itself, and all of these parts were there at the beginning. There are no new parts, just parts of the *all that always was*, reforming itself into what looks like new and different parts of the *all that is*. This is a strange and difficult concept to understand, and may be better understood if it is visualised as a type of *lava lamp*. The coloured wax within the clear liquid of the glass container, when heated by the hot bulb underneath rises up, and then cools, falling as different pieces, before reforming itself and rising again. All of the wax is one piece, which is constantly reforming itself.

The individual parts of this soul, and indeed the whole soul itself, produce *thought energy*. This thought energy vibrates to produce *spirit matter*, which slows down changing its vibration to produce matter - the slower the vibration, the denser the matter.

We can therefore think of life energy as conscious thought, and universal wisdom as *Divine Consciousness*.

Our views of Divine consciousness have changed over time and bring up strong emotions. There are those who are so adamant in their views that they will not change, and others who are searching for their own truths. It could be said that religion encourages you to explore the thoughts of others, and accept them as your own, whereas spirituality invites you to discover your own truths. Whatever views you hold, for the most part they do bring up strong emotions, which leads us to the question. What are emotions?

Human emotions are complex psycho physiological experiences, in other words the *state of mind*. Emotions involve physiological arousal, expressive behaviour and conscious experience. They are influenced by the environment and produce biochemical reactions within the body.

This environment is not just the natural environment, but also the surroundings in which an individual lives. Emotions are associated with mood, temperament, personality, disposition and motivation. Although motivation directs and energises behavior, emotions provide the affective component to motivation - in other words a positive or negative feeling.

There are five natural emotions, love, fear, anger, envy and grief.

There is really only one true emotion and that is love. Everything is an expression of love in its highest form. When love is freely expressed, given and received without any conditions, it brings joy and happiness, spreading kindness, compassion and affection. It is the energy which expands shares and heals. There are many forms of love, and when this love is repressed or becomes difficult to express, and leads to fear.

Fear is a distressing negative sensation arising from a perceived threat or danger. It has two main responses *fight* or *flight*. Fear almost always relates to a future event which is the cause of anxiety. It can also arise from an instant reaction to something happening in the present. As children we initially experience no fear as we are innocent and live in a state of love. It is only when we encounter a perceived threat or danger that we leave our state of love and descend into fear. Fear can be described as **F**alse **E**vidence **A**ppearing **R**eal, and leads to caution. Fear is the energy which contracts, hides, and harms.

Anger is the emotion that allows you to say *no thank you*, and does not have to be abusive or damaging. However, if repressed it becomes rage. Anger is an emotion related to a feeling of being offended, wronged or denied. It involves the strong and uncomfortable emotional response to a perceived provocation, in other words the loss of control of a situation.

Normally there is nothing wrong in saying *no thank you* in a positive way, as we all have a free choice to decline something. Anger is usually perceived as being pressure building up inside until it explodes into rage. This rage can be extremely intense, and lasts until a perceived threat is removed or the person experiencing it is incapacitated. It is again fear based, and is at the opposite end of the spectrum to love. Depression can also increase the chances of experiencing feelings of rage.

Depression seriously affects thoughts, behavior, and physical well-being. It may also include feelings of sadness, anxiety, emptiness, hopelessness, worthlessness, guilt, and also cause irritability and restlessness. This low state of being leads to lethargy where there is a loss of interest in activities which were once pleasurable. It also leads to loss of concentration, memory, and decision making ability. In its worse form it can also lead to suicide. It is a direct reaction to certain events, and again is fear based and is often preceded by grief.

Envy is a natural emotion urging us to strive for more. There is nothing wrong in observing that someone has achieved more and wishing to emulate them. It is the trigger to work harder at what we do to raise our standards of living, or academic achievement. When used positively it can be a good thing. However, if it is repressed it can lead to a feeling of inadequacy. This inadequacy can lead to low self esteem, and this combined with a feeling of lack, can lead to jealousy.

Jealousy is fear driven, and instead of encouraging us to strive for more in a positive way, it descends into bitterness. This bitterness instead of encouraging a desire to improve is very negative and quickly builds into resentment, which in turn leads to anger. If jealousy is not kept in check, then it destroys, whereas envy creates.

There is another emotion which is probably one of the most difficult to express and that is one of forgiveness. It takes great strength and courage to forgive someone who has wronged you. If you are able to do this then it releases you from fear, and it will no longer haunt you, like a ghost in a haunted house.

From my own near death experiences I have discovered that there is really no such place as hell, or such a thing as evil, it is merely a concept generated by the human mind. It is a concept of fear which counterbalances love. In order to experience love you have to have the opposite - fear. There is no such thing as good or bad either, only love. In order to know what love is you have to have fear, to experience it!

Love is the coming together of two parts of the many parts of the one soul, combining into one part of the many parts instinctively combining without fear, anger, envy or grief.

Our emotions are very important and give us a sense of how we feel at a given moment in time. However, time is not really what it seems to be. All events that you could possibly imagine or have imagined are taking place right *now*. This is the moment that precedes your awareness. It is what is happening before the light gets to you. This is the present moment sent to you, created by you, before you ever know it. This is referred to as the present, or now. You have the ability to choose which one of these experiences you have imagined, and by choosing it you are experiencing it *now*.

We are living in an illusion, and what we are looking at is not what we are really seeing. Your brain is not the source of your intelligence, merely the data processor. It takes in information through receptors called your *senses*. It interprets this energy information according to its previous data on the subject. It then tells you what it perceives, not what really is. Based on these perceptions you think you know the truth about something when in reality you are creating the events yourself. Life is the process by which everything is being created in pure energy, which is being transmuted into matter. This pure energy is what we call *life*, and it is our awareness of this which is the process by which all is created and experienced by itself.

Everything you see and feel in the *Heavens* and on *Earth* is actually *The Divine* being *created*. This process of being created is eternal, and everything is forever being created. Nothing is without movement, and everything is energy in motion. This energy motion can also be called *emotion*, which in turn is called *life*.

When we think about the word human being, it is simply a human *being*, and this being is referred to as living in the *now*.

This information is all very well, but on practical terms very few of us live in what is termed as the *now*. What is meant by the *now* is being enlightened and rising above thought. We are all thinking about something most of the time and develop a mental image of ourselves. This image is often referred to as the *ego*, and is the result of life experience. It is mostly concerned about keeping the past alive, and considering the future. It desires only one thing, *survival*, and convinces itself that, if certain things happen then everything will turn out well in the end. It therefore only considers the present as a means to this end.

When you listen to your thoughts, you can hear a deeper presence somewhere behind them. It is this deeper presence or internal guidance that is living in the *now*. Alternating between the thoughts and this presence enables you to be in the moment, as opposed to being in the past or future. By just emptying your mind of all thoughts and just listening to the sounds around you, taking in the smells, and noticing those everyday things that you normally pass by, and letting your senses guide you, you can experience the *now*.

Senses are what we use to perceive things. Human beings have six main senses which are sight, hearing, taste, smell, touch and psychic perception. The last of these senses enables us to connect to something beyond our normal physical experiences. We all have this ability, and it is only a question of developing it. It could be compared to a lazy muscle that improves in strength with exercise. In essence it is the ability to see, hear or feel a presence from the *spirit world*. This perception is something that everyone has experienced at some point in their lives, be it in the waking state or through a dream.

In other words, your feelings are your truths. What is best for you is what is true for you. Thoughts are not feelings they are ideas of how you should feel. When thoughts and feelings get confused, truth becomes clouded. Once you know your truth, live it!

Negative feelings are not true feelings at all, they are just thoughts about something based on previous experiences. They are not truth as *truth* is created in the *now*. The past and future can only exist as thoughts. There is no such thing as *hell*, the *devil*, or *purgatory*, these are only thoughts too. *Heaven* does exist, although it is not quite what we imagine it to be.

We are a complex coalition of three component parts. First there is the *mind*, which actually exists in every cell of the body, the brain being just the processor. It is hard to imagine that in fact 99% of the body is actually empty space. The second part is the *body*, which is the vessel which carries the mind and soul/spirit. The third and most important part is the *spirit/soul*. The soul exists in the empty space within the body, and in the auric field.

For those who are not aware of the *auric field*, it is an energy field which surrounds the human body. It can be seen by psychics and photographed by a *kirlian* camera. The camera is named after *Semyon Kirlian* who in 1939 accidentally discovered that if he connected a voltage to a photographic plate the image showed the energy fields around the human body. These energy fields look like layers of coloured energy, and these colours represent the emotional state of the person being photographed at that given moment.

The soul is actually the container for the body, the soul of the *Divine* holds in the universe, and the soul of *Man* holds each individual human body.

All three component parts live in a coalition and each has its own identity. The soul exists in the body, where it relinquishes its freedom in order to be contained within the body. When the body is asleep the soul leaves to recharge its proverbial *batteries*. On certain occasions the soul can also leave the body in a waking state. This out of body experiences is referred to as *consciousness raising*.

This consciousness raising is very similar to when we pass over. What we perceive as our individual soul has the free choice as to which new life it would like to choose. It can re-enter the same body and take up where it left off, to enter a new body, or to remain in the cosmic grid, or maybe briefly enter the state of *Nirvana*.

When someone has passed over, by just thinking of them you can establish a connection. Sometime you may recognise a sign given by them. It may be a fleeting glance of them out of the corner of your eye, and yet, when you turn the vision has gone. An item connected to them may mysteriously appear, or be impossible to find. You may even feel a warm glow in your heart. The most important thing is that there is no such thing as death, as all life is eternal. It is the start of the next part of the journey, although for the ones left behind it is in no way as joyful an experience.

We wish our loved ones to remain with us in good health so that we can enjoy their company, and seek their advice and support. We miss not having them near us, and it is really us being needy. They are free of all emotions except love. Love is the part of us which enables us to live through the heart with only the purest of emotions, and it is transmuted into euphoric love. From my own experiences, when you are freed from the human body you can be what you want to be, go where you want to go, and do as much of everything as you wish all at the same time.

The dream state is the nearest that we can normally experience this, and living in the now we can also experience what it feels like to be in our light body. The light body is our pure energy state, and it can not only be seen, but also manipulated.

Life can therefore now be understood in terms of thoughts and emotions governed by consciousness, and this consciousness has already eloquently been defined by *Rene Descartes* as *I think therefore I am*.

You do not necessarily have to be asleep to experience the dream state, as the process of *Hypnosis* - which is an altered state of mind, closely resembles this. It is a form of unconsciousness, which decreases your peripheral awareness shifting your attention from the surrounding and what physical sensation you are experiencing, to a deeper level of awareness. This deeper level of awareness is accessed by inducing a state of physical relaxation where anxiety, confidence and low self esteem can be improved by getting to the root of the problem, and identifying the cause.

It is also a form of *spiritually healing*. Your body has a spirit, and your spirit or soul lives multiple lives. It is often within a past life where the problems you have been experiencing in this life originate.

This is a controversial subject, as many people deny the very concepts of *re-incarnation*. They believe that once you have died your life is over and there is nothing that follows. They do not believe in past lives, and refute any evidence of those who have experienced other lifetimes. There are many documented cases, particularly of children who describe the lives that they once lived, where they lived, and who their families were. Instead of being attributed to a vivid imagination on further examination evidence of their accounts have been proven true.

Hypnotism is a process of enabling access to these memories by regressing back into a past life by going through your soul's records, and finding the past life connected with the problems that your are experiencing in this lifetime.

We are all conscious of, and experience our surroundings by using our senses. This information is stored for future reference, and this process has been going on in all of our previous lives and will keep going in future lives too. All of this information is stored in a place often referred to as our *higher consciousness*.

On a physical level, the gland which allows us to have these visions in our minds during hypnosis is called the *Pineal Gland*. This gland has all of the components of an eye inside it, which is why it is often referred to as the *third eye*. The outside of it looks like a regular blob of brain tissue, and produces DMT (Dimethyltryptamine), which is the chemical that allows a soul to live in a body. A baby produces DMT in the womb from the 49th day after conception, which is the movement and brainwaves start.

Accessing the Pineal Gland can not only be achieved by hypnosis, certain narcotic substances can also stimulate it and cause hallucinations. These *hallucinations* can often be very unpleasant and not linked to past lives at all. On other occasions they can be similar to daydreaming, where you create the vision you want.

One question which always arises is that of why we cannot remember our past lives?

If we were able to do this, then we could learn so much and derive great benefit from all of this information. The main reason that we cannot remember is that we are here to experience, and these *experiences* are dictated by what we did in the past - in other words *Karma*.

For every event that occurs, there will follow another event whose existence is caused by the first, and this second event will be pleasant or unpleasant according to its cause. Karma is not punishment for what you do, but rather another tool you use to learn.

You own your karma, are born of it, related to it, live supported by it, and whatever karma you create, whether good or bad, you inherit it.

In this lifetime, when you show negativity, your DNA will coil up, and start to deteriorate and slowly break down. When you show love, your DNA will expand, straighten, and strengthen. When dealing with Karma, it is not about being punished for the things that you have done in the past, it is about learning from the mistakes that you made. It is more about showing love and being positive, and releasing negativity which has accumulated over time.

Sometimes, when undergoing hypnosis, it may not be the exact past life which is accessed - in some cases it may be a metaphor. These *metaphors* help you to gain a meaning from that situation and help you to resolve the situation which is causing you problems in this lifetime.

It is also possible to go forward to future lifetimes, and this process is referred to a *progression*. However, this is not always accurate as there are an infinite number of possibilities that may occur in the future. This brings us to the concept of *Parallel universes*. All of these other possibilities exist alongside each other, and it is your own *free will* that enables you to choose exactly which one to take. Every decision you take opens up yet another set of possibilities, just like travelling on a road with an infinite set of junctions. Each time that you make a turn you alter your own future.

So what part does Luke play in all of this, and why have I experienced a large part of his life?

This is the question that I have been asking myself ever since he made his first appearance.

For a start, he appeared at a time in my life when I was seeking answers. He also appeared when I was in need, especially when there were strange *goings ons!*

His strength and courage gave me strength and the courage to battle on, and battle is what it was for many years, particularly with my illness. In some ways I feel as though my mother's wisdom is reflected in the Sultan who introduced Luke to his library, in the same way my own mother taught me how to read and write and guided me so very well. Her council is something that I deeply miss as her wisdom along with all of her other wonderful qualities, is something that I will never be able to replace.

The king reminds me of my beloved father who was in my eyes like a king. His strength was legendary and his sense of justice unequalled. He was to all of us like a castle, whose walls protected us from harm, and if ever there was a knight in shining armour then it was he.

I do not have a brother, however for many years I always felt as though I was playing *second fiddle*, as I struggled at school, being profoundly dyslexic. I also felt that I was *out of step* with most peoples thinking and felt differently about most things. I could never go along with the *crowd*, having to do my own thing in my own peculiar way!

I have never been comfortable with religion, or churches for that matter, even though I have met some wonderful people who have had a strong connection to them. I just thought that I was a little strange, although with some of the *colourful* characters I have met, maybe I am not quite as strange as I thought!

It is ironic that the love of my life is also beautiful, tall slim with hazel eyes containing golden flecks and flowing blonde hair. I first met Catherine on a course, where we sat next to each other, shared body language, and even the same glass of water by accident. When we got into conversation we found out that we had lived off the same road for years. When I lived in Solihull, her office was at the end of the next road, I then spent some time in America, and so did she. We both returned and moved to Chester, where I co-owned a recording studio (misspent youth!) and she lived off the same road. I then sold my share, and acquired a manager with hopes of a career as a recoding artist. She moved house and now lived on the same road as my manager. I then became ill and had to give up my aspirations, and her business career now involved dealing with supermarkets. I used to shop in the same one she dealt with, and my mother actually started talking to her and introduced me to her. We were both a little embarrassed at my mother's match making!

After the sad loss of my parents I moved to South Warrington, and again lived off the same road. Catherine had seen some of my artwork advertised locally and wished to purchase one of my pictures and was just waiting for the right time to call. I was asked to take some of my artwork to the course we attended, and the one of particular interest to her was of a mermaid. The space she had in mind would only take a landscape picture, and the one advertised was portrait. I created this new version and was never able to sell the original landscape version. Even the top she was wearing was the same colours as the picture, and the picture looks just like her. In fact, everyone thinks that it is her!

I even had many dreams of a beautiful tall slim woman with striking green eyes and flowing blonde hair ever since Luke made his first appearance. Catherine on the other hand spent some time with the Native Americans who told her that she would be with someone with the same description as myself.

We feel as though we have always been together, and think and feel the same about practically everything. Even whist out shopping we have emerged from different parts of the same store carrying the exact same item. We really are as one!

The only thing that I do not share with Luke is his temper - my pen is indeed mightier than his sword. Perhaps that is the Karmic lesson I have learnt in this lifetime, or perhaps I had to come back to live in a time where I could search out my answers without having to do battle.

Being profoundly dyslexic as a child, I was not able to read at all. Looking back, I now realise that on a soul level I was preventing myself from reading about others interpretations of life, having chosen to experience them for myself. I also chose my own parents - one thing that I did get right!

They were magnificent in every way and allowed me the time and space to *be*, and to experience life under their guidance and protection. I think it is safe to say that I have had many experiences, and met a lot of very *colourful* characters.

My wonderful mother taught me how to read and write, and without her I would not have been able to write this book. Ironically, at one stage in my life I had actually written more books than I had read!

I know that Luke is a very important part of my life and maybe his love of books has enabled me to become an author?

He taught me many things such as you have to experience bad, to know what is good. He also taught me that life is eternal and that the times may change, but our own respective journeys are very similar in many ways. Sometimes I did wish that I had his sword in my hand although he realised that the true power lies within. I am Luke and Luke is part of me, as we are connected, as we all are connected because we all share the same soul which has been divided countless times. Is he part of my imagination?

The answer to this question is *yes*, as we and everything else in this universe of ours are all nothing more than thoughts.

Did he really exist?

Well, I think that he did. Maybe he was not quite the man I saw in the visions as they had to be processed through my own emotions and perceptions. What I can say for certain is that there are men of conviction who stay true to their principles and embark on journeys of discovery. What he discovered in the end was that all there is, is love, and to love yourself, your fellow man and to carry that love in your heart is all that really matters.

Thankfully I am now fit and well, really happy, showered in love and plenty of understanding from my wonderful soul mate Catherine and her equally wonderful parents, and thrilled at not only being alive, but in having the opportunity to do what I love. For all of this I give my heartfelt thanks.

Oh, and as for my phobia of storms - I still have it, although it is not quite as bad as it was. It could well be connected to another past life, and if that is the case then there will probably be another adventure awaiting me...